"Allison and Piper show immense ... story. Anyone who has experience with someone with a mental illness can connect to the feelings of guilt, worry, and shame. *Unconditional* reminds us that we are not alone in these feelings, while providing exercises and steps for moving forward when you love someone with a mental illness."

-Mackenzie Wissink, Child Behavior Interventionist

"A must read for all! *Unconditional* is a raw, riveting, and vulnerable portrayal of one mother and daughter's emotional journey through the realities of adolescent depression and the disappointing failure of the systems around them. Weaved throughout their journey are priceless nuggets of knowledge and insight, including compassionate, empowering ways to move forward that inspire hope and healing."

-Kelli Saginak, EdD, Professor, Life, Weight, and Functional Health Coach

"*Unconditional* is a jolt to the system. Allison and Piper's deep genuineness and vulnerability is a much needed companion for any parent, especially those feeling lost and scared learning to cope with their child's mental health struggles. Their accurate and eye opening insights stopped me in my tracks and caused me to take a deeper look in how I can better support my clients and my own children. *Unconditional* is a must for your bibliotherapy library."

-Jack Hinman, Executive Director
Moonridge Academy

unconditional

Allison & Piper Garner

unconditional

Learning to Navigate
& Reframe Mental Illness
— TOGETHER —

NEW YORK

LONDON • NASHVILLE • MELBOURNE • VANCOUVER

Unconditional

Learning to Navigate and Reframe Mental Illness – Together

Published in New York, New York, by Morgan James Publishing. Morgan James is a trademark of Morgan James, LLC. www.MorganJamesPublishing.com

ISBN 9781642798784 paperback
ISBN 9781642798791 eBook
Library of Congress Control Number: 2019952540

Cover Design by:
Rachel Lopez
www.r2cdesign.com

Interior Design by:
Christopher Kirk
www.GFSstudio.com

Author Photos by:
Laurie Marie

Morgan James is a proud partner of Habitat for Humanity Peninsula and Greater Williamsburg. Partners in building since 2006.

Get involved today! Visit
MorganJamesPublishing.com/giving-back

Contents

Introduction

I am frustrated. My daughter suffers from depression and distorted thinking, and I can't make it stop. The mental health systems we have in place don't work for her. The medications don't seem to make a significant difference. Her therapists don't seem to be able to make much forward progress.

She finds it difficult to make and keep friends. Nobody really wants to talk about self-harm, eating disorders, suicide, anxiety, and depression. I don't feel like anyone really gets it.

I wish there was a better way.

In a moment of desperation, after our adolescent daughter, Piper's, second suicide attempt and hospitalization, I wondered why there wasn't a book that had been written by a mother who had been through this. What an amazing book that would be. I would buy that book!

So, I decided to write a book about the journey of parenting a child who lives in a dark place, a place that is difficult to escape.

As part of her journey through this, my daughter uses journaling as a coping tool to regulate herself and was wholeheartedly willing to contribute some of her entries to this book. You'll find them scattered through the chapters—an offer of her honest thoughts in some of her darkest moments. She said that if this book could help just one other girl like her, then it will have been worth exposing those scary and troubling thoughts to the world.

So, here it is. Our dirty laundry—what it's like for a mother to parent an emotionally unstable teen and how it feels to be an adolescent struggling with the emotional roller coaster of severe depression.

For those of you who are reading this because you are in the midst of crisis, please know that you are who this book is for. My daughter and I hope that this book is useful to other mothers and daughters (fathers and sons too!) experiencing similar challenges. We stand with you in spirit as you travel your journey, and we want you to know that you are not alone in this emotional tornado.

Section I

Helpful Mindsets

Chapter 1

Suicide is Not the Answer

My thoughts about suicide have gone back and forth dramatically through the course of our family's journey. Before our daughter began suffering from depression, I just felt bad for the families who had to live through the aftermath of losing a member to suicide. Secretly, I thanked God that I would never have to deal with that because my kids and spouse were A-OK. It was always this tragedy seen and pitied from a distance—until one day it wasn't.

My daughter came into my room one night after I'd gone to bed. My husband was out of town, and she was frantic and scared and uttered those terrible words that strike fear and terror into any parent's heart: "Mom, I want to kill myself."

Uncomfortable Truth

There I was, in that moment, wondering how the heck we'd come to this place. How is my daughter, at only twelve years old, thinking about suicide? What could be so terrible in her life that dying seemed like the next step? What kind of pain was she experiencing? And the big one … What kind of mother had I been to create such a daughter?

I immediately went into triage mode. I told her to crawl into bed with me and reassured her—and myself—that she would be okay. Nothing in this world is so bad that dying is the answer.

Then I tucked her right next to me and hoped that a good night's rest would settle her worried mind. A few hours later, I felt her getting out of the bed. I rolled over and asked where she was going, and, as it turns out, she was sneaking out of my room to grab all the pills in the medicine cabinet and run away to take them and die in peace. This was serious. This was unbelievable. This was our new reality.

Just the threat of suicide can rock a family to its core, and it did for us. Suddenly, I was the head sentry who was *always* on guard. I worried about leaving her home alone. We locked away all the pills and sharp objects in the house. But I started to wonder what we would do if she eventually found a way to succeed. To date, she's had five hospitalizations and three suicide attempts. And all we can do is play it by ear, one day, one moment at a time.

Steep Learning Curve

Her first suicide attempt felt like a Hallmark movie special, and not in a good way. I found myself on the phone with Poison Control, who directed me to take my daughter to the ER immediately. No sooner had we arrived at the hospital than she was given twelve ounces of some black (seriously, black) liquid. They explained, "This is charcoal. You need to drink *all* of it. Now. It tastes terrible and it's really gritty. Good luck."

My daughter shuddered with each swallow and, after about thirty minutes, she still hadn't ingested it all. She didn't really care if the medicines she had swallowed destroyed her kidneys, liver, or stomach lining. With an IV sticking out of her arm and an insane amount of cords surrounding her, I just kept asking myself what had happened to my baby.

The second suicide attempt happened when she was admitted to an inpatient program at a behavioral health hospital. I received a call after dinner from a nurse who was working with our daughter that evening. He calmly (yes, calmly) informed me that our daughter had left a group therapy session visibly upset, so they let her go to her room. After about twenty minutes, the staff went to check on her and found her choking herself with her sweatshirt. My adrenaline shot through the roof and my mind started to spin out of control. I couldn't comprehend how we had gotten here, to this place where my daughter was in a mental hospital trying to kill herself. What the heck was going on? And how could we make this all stop?

The third attempt was a lot like her first. Yes, we locked up all the medications in the house, but she was able to squeeze her small hand into our cabinets and find a bottle of pills. She happened to grab her own antidepressants and swallowed all of them. When I noticed her acting differently and asked what was wrong, she told me what she'd done. It felt like Groundhog Day. Call Poison Control. Drive to the ER. Get the charcoal. Vomit profusely. Monitor vitals for four hours. Send her to another psych ward.

So now, suicide is no longer a thing that happens to other families. It now lives in our home. We are among the families that worry about what we will find when we come home, or get up in the morning, or pick up our daughter at school. We are the ones who have locks on our cabinets. We are the ones who don't sleep at night because of the worry and dread hanging over our heads. We are the ones desperate to find relief for our child in a world that treats mental illness as an infectious and shameful disease. We are the ones who take our child to doctors, psychiatrists, therapists, hospitals, ER's, dieticians, day treatments, and school counselors in an effort to find answers and support. We are the ones who sheepishly walk into the doors of a National Alliance on Mental Illness (NAMI) meeting hoping to find just one other person who might understand what we are going through.

It's not them anymore. It's us.

Suicide Is Permanent

Eight years ago, our family survived the crisis that accompanies addiction, so I have firsthand knowledge of the destruction that can be left behind from something like that. A single family member's decisions have the power to send shock waves through the entire family.

Just like our experience living with addiction, I have no doubt that a successful suicide attempt would ravage our family, our lives, and our community. We'd be left to pick up the pieces and find the will to move on. And I'm not sure we would be able to do that. I've watched other families in the aftermath of a death of a child, and what I've seen is not good. Siblings blame themselves and parents resent each other. Everyone is angry and scared and lost. It's a hurricane that rips through the soul of each and every member of a family.

Recognizing that our daughter's behavior is a means to avoiding her painful thoughts and emotions helps me stay grounded during these terrifying events, during the times when I do start thinking about what a successful attempt might do to our family. She isn't crazy. She isn't careless. She isn't selfish. But she is in pain. And she wants it to stop.

If only our daughter could believe that everything is temporary: pain, pleasure, sadness, joy. We all know how it feels when we hurt, and there are times when I, too, would've gone to extremes to make the pain stop. But the obvious problem with suicide is its permanence. Once it's done, there is no going back. All the wonderful and terrible moments that are still to come are stolen. Recovery from the pain is erased. The path through the darkness stands empty— forever.

If my daughter ever succeeds in killing herself, then I know for certain she is killing a part of each of us too. Watching helplessly as a loved one suffers is an intense and relentless torture. Every one of us wants our suffering to end. However, suicide doesn't end anyone's pain, not really. While the person who is gone might no longer be actively suffering, a new kind of agony arises for those left behind. We would wonder what we could have done differently and question who and what is to blame. We would fall into a dark hole ourselves as we grieve. And we would never be the same. Because suicide would kill us too, only more slowly, more insidiously, more cruelly.

Words from Piper

Suicide may end the emotional pain, but it starts ten times more pain then there was in the first place. For example, when you end your life you are being selfish, I was being selfish when I took those pills. When you try to end your life, you are also ending happiness and families. Your family will hurt, they will hurt a lot more than you could ever imagine. Your family will be torn apart because of an impulsive move you made. So, yes, suicide may end your pain, but it starts a lot of other people's pain too.

So, what do you do then? If you can't end your life, then how do you stop the pain? You start to try, you put work into it, and you try to get better. You try to be happy, and you will fail a lot, but that doesn't matter because one day you will look back and think that it was all worth it to keep going. So, don't stop now, don't take your life now. Get better and get happy.

When I Took the Pills

When I took the pills, I felt like there was no way out except to take the pills and die. After I took them, I instantly felt a rush of fear devour me. I had made a huge mistake. I called my mom. My hands were shaking, and I could barely hold the phone. I felt so guilty. Why would I try to hurt everyone by doing this? How could I be so selfish to think that no one cared about me? The texts started to roll in, text after text "piper are you okay?" "no" "no stop omg" "piper talk to me". They all cared, and I was so self-centered that I couldn't take a step back to look and see how great my life could be going. All I cared about was myself and I sat around all day feeling so sorry for myself when I could've been having a good life and going out and making new friends. I was mad at myself. Why did I take the pills? Why did I do it? I kept asking myself over and over again. The answer was that I did not want the pain anymore. I just wanted it all to stop. And, in the moment, that was the only thing I thought I could do to make the pain stop. I was wrong. There was so much help around me, and I never reached out to anyone.

Suicide Can be an Attempt to End Several Things

Suicide can be an attempt to end several things. First, the pain. If you are overwhelmed with feelings and thoughts, you think suicide may be the only way to end it for you. But it's not. Second, it can be an attempt to show people how much they hurt you. If someone you loved hurts you enough, you may feel that they need to see how much they hurt you. Third, it can be an attempt to end the voices. If you hear voices or see things or even feel things that aren't there, it can be a way to get away from the fantasy life that you have been living and never have to worry about the voices or the things you may see.

Many Illnesses Can Cause Suicidal Thoughts

There are so many illnesses that can cause suicidal thoughts but a few of them cause more severe thoughts than others. For example, depression can be very severe and cause suicidal thoughts because of the numbness you may feel when you have depression. Also, you can feel very worthless with depression, which could cause you to think that suicide is the only way out of your pain. Eating disorders *can cause suicidal thoughts for a few different reasons. First off, when your health is at a low point from not eating or purging, it can cause suicidal thoughts because your brain and body aren't functioning right anymore. Another way eating disorders can cause suicidal thoughts is by thinking you are too fat or that suicide is a way to punish yourself because you feel like you ate way too much or because you gained weight.*

Is It a Way to Seek Attention?

A suicide attempt can be a way to look for attention because the person may feel like no one cares and they need to get people to care so they can get through the pain. It could also be a test to see who would care if I were to do this? Who actually loves me?

Don't Get Upset with Someone Who Has Attempted Suicide

Instead of getting mad or disappointed with someone who has tried committing suicide or is having suicidal thoughts, be there for them. Help them. Get them what they need because I can tell you from personal experience that it sucks when people get mad at you or call you names because you are hurting. Think about the person and think about why they would ever think to end their life. It's because they are in pain and the sooner you can stop the pain the better it will be. Think about them and not yourself, don't be selfish because you're scared. Learn to live with the fear and get through the fear. Learn how to not lash out at someone else because of your own feelings. Talk about it *because that is what is the most helpful. Yes, there will be a lot of trust broken and there will be new strict rules. No, it's not because they don't love you. It's because they **do** love you. If they didn't love you, they wouldn't put the time in to help you and make sure you are safe at home.*

Steps for Moving Forward:

1. Talk about suicide and depression without judgment with your children. If they share their own or another's suicidal thoughts with you, listen to them. While you may panic on the inside, it is important to create a safe space for your child to discuss this terrifying subject.
2. Model self-care for your children. Take time to do things that relax and rejuvenate you.

Exercises:

1. Ask your family members to share three things they are grateful for each evening at the dinner table. Gratitude is a great way to develop emotional resilience.
2. Talk to the unconscious part of your child's brain. Share a story about someone else who experienced something you think your kid is currently experiencing.

Chapter 2

Shame and Blame Must Go

I f there is anything we have learned about dealing with emotional difficulties, it's that shame and blame greatly hinder our progress. When we hear something that distresses us about a loved one, we tend to look for people to blame and systems to point fingers at. At a time when resources and support are critical, shame and blame will throw us off course and prolong suffering for everyone involved.

Dreaded Phone Call

We say that we love our children unconditionally. But is it true? Can we really say that? Is it too hard sometimes? Do we find that we love our children when they do things that we like and are disappointed when they do things we don't like? And then do we get upset with them when they do things we *really* don't like?

At the end of the day, if we don't like what our children are doing, it's usually because we are scared. We are letting fear drive our thoughts and dictate our reactions. What would it look like to truly love a child unconditionally, through and past our own fears?

One day, I got a phone call from my daughter's day treatment therapist. She shared with me that my daughter was having a lot of anxiety and was not feeling confident that she could keep herself safe. They asked me if I could provide twenty-four-hour supervision, and I agreed. Then they asked me if I could lock up all the medicines since she mentioned feeling like taking them and hurting herself. Again, I agreed. Then they asked me if I could prevent her from running away since she mentioned feeling like drowning herself or jumping in front of a train. At that point, I did not agree. I could envision lots of ways for her to sneak out of the house and I didn't feel confident that I could prevent her from doing so. The result was that she was sent straight to the emergency room to be admitted into an inpatient program.

I was heartbroken. We had gone without a single hospitalization in a month—our longest stint in over three months. Just when we felt like we had her on the right track and she was climbing out of her dark hole, she seemed powerless to continue her upward climb. In those moments, all I want to do is reach down, grab her hand, and pull her out of the hole myself. Of course, that isn't possible, nor would it help her to learn to climb out herself. So, my husband escorted her to the queue of the mentally ill and had her admitted in about three hours.

As I anxiously waited at home for more information, I had the following text exchange with my daughter.

Piper: "I'm sorry mom. I blew it and I wish I didn't. I'm regretting myself sooo much for not trying to be safe. I'm sorry."

Me: "Oh honey. Don't apologize. We are learning! I love you!!!"

Piper: "I love you too. Being here and remembering how much I hated it made me realize that if I put in the work I can stay safe at home and I wish I could've realized that sooner before it was too late."

Me: "It's never too late. C'mon home!"

Piper: "I wish it was that easy, I did come to the ER voluntarily which means if by tomorrow or any other day you feel you can trust me to be home you can discharge me."

Me: "Ok. That'll work. Please don't worry! (heart emoticons)"

When the fear sets in, it's hard to be present and do what is needed in the moment. I don't know what I need, what she needs, what to do, where to be, what to ask for. I become this mess of fear and worry and catastrophizing. I think about how many hospital visits we have left to endure before she'll get better. I worry that this cycle will never end. I fear that she'll never be able to recover and will continue to suffer forever. I wonder what we are missing that is so obviously plaguing her and think if we could just figure it out, she can end the agony.

When I let fear get in the driver's seat, I experience feelings of despair, frustration, and disappointment. Even if I say I am not feeling those things, my daughter will know it isn't true. She is an empath, as are all children, and can sense the real truth. She might feel as though my love for her is conditional if I become disappointed when she cannot manage her emotional turmoil. She may feel betrayed or ashamed or both. She may hear my words reassuring her that I am fine, but she'll know deep down that it's untrue and she won't be able to trust me. She'll feel unworthy and unlovable.

That kind of conditional love is dangerous. It can drive family members farther from each other at a time when it's critical to stand together. To love my daughter unconditionally means setting my fear aside. It means asking myself what the path forward looks like and tapping into my compassionate self for what will most help my daughter. Typically, the path forward looks like my daughter traveling this journey and experiencing the consequences of her decisions so she can learn. My heart—my compassion—tells me to stand beside her on this journey, supporting her and loving her through the pain without judgment or disappointment.

Together, my rationale and compassion help me step around my fear, acknowledging it and letting it go, to become present for what is happening in the moment. That's how my unconditional love can flow through me to her. It releases me from judgment, shame, and blame, which, in turn, releases her too.

First Shame Memory

When I pull up my first memory of being ashamed, the one that comes forward is wetting the bed as a child. I was an occasional bed wetter until about ten years old. It was a huge source of embarrassment for me because, at some point, I learned that it was rare to still be wetting the bed at "my age." After one bed wetting event, I remember waking up my mom in the middle of the night so she could change my sheets. She cursed under her breath and groggily shuffled into my room. She seemed really angry as she ripped my dirty sheets from my bed and replaced them with dry ones. She didn't say anything that I can remember, but I recall feeling like I was the source of her anger. And I remember deciding that night to never tell her that I wet the bed again.

Instead of telling my mom, I would air out my mattress and sheets each time I wet the bed. I would pull back the sheets so they could get some air flow and pull up the fitted sheet so the mattress would dry. It all seemed like a perfectly good solution to a child. But even though my sheets and mattress did eventually dry, of course the stench of urine didn't go away. So, I would hope that my mom didn't go in my room for days at a time so that she wouldn't find out I had wet the bed again.

Now, I didn't feel like I had *done* something wrong when I wet the bed. Instead, I felt like I *was* wrong because I still wet the bed. That assumption and my negative belief were validated by my mom's negative reaction. As children, we tend to assume that we are responsible for our parent's moods and behaviors, so I never even questioned whether her annoyance and frustration had anything to do with me; I was certain it did.

And that small instance, one my mom might not even remember, is how shame started for me and how I carried shame forward into the rest of my life. My assumptions about other people's reactions only fueled my shame and had me hiding all sorts of things I thought made me a bad person. Still, at the age of forty-four,

I assumed my daughter had mental illness because I was a bad mom. Instead of focusing on my daughter's needs, I was focusing on hiding my faults, preventing my shame like I was that ten-year-old girl airing out her sheets again.

When I finally discovered that my parenting might not be the reason my daughter was suffering (Hint: *your* parenting is not the reason your child is suffering), it was such a big relief. I could get her the help she needed, because I no longer felt the sting of shame and embarrassment when I spoke about her challenges. I could speak with teachers, principals, parents, therapists, doctors, nurses, my clients, friends, and family—all without being sheepish or humiliated. My own issues with shame had been blocking me from getting my daughter what she needed, so the sooner I could ditch those assumptions, the sooner we could get around to focusing on getting better.

Carrying That Which Isn't Mine

When our daughter began to struggle emotionally, it was easy for me to chalk it up to puberty, teenage angst, or a poor choice of friends. It was a simple approach, but it worked for a while—until things got worse. Then we had to look inside the home to things like social media usage, parenting decisions, and relationships in the family. I found myself judging other parents harshly and wondering how their kids were "normal" when I was a much better parent and my kid wasn't "normal." I felt confused, discouraged, and self-conscious, wrapped up in this comparison mode.

Finding resolution for my daughter's issues was my top priority. I took control of everything. I began enrolling her in different programs to work on her anxiety and depression. I got her a therapist so she could talk through her issues and find coping skills. I found her a psychiatrist so we could start administering the proper medications. I controlled her weekly and weekend schedules, what foods she ate, which friends she hung out with, her homework, her clothing … well, you get the idea. In my mind, there was nothing in *her* suffering that I couldn't overcome. Cue Superwoman music.

Here's the rub: the more I controlled, the worse our relationship became. My daughter was already feeling out of control with all of her thoughts and emotions constantly swirling about. When I tried to take the reins, she lost yet another level of control, which only exacerbated the issues. Not only was I not helping, I was making things worse for her. My assumption that a "good mother" would be able to fix her daughter was being turned upside down.

Looking back, I can see that my motivations didn't ultimately stem from trying to be a "good mother." Deep down, I was disgraced that our daughter was not "normal." To assuage my discomfort, I jumped right in to "fix" her so that I wouldn't have to feel that way anymore. I was carrying my daughter's issues on my back, which didn't serve either of us. Instead, it was pulling us apart and keeping us from working together. When I relinquished control and let my daughter determine her own needs, I found that I learned a lot more, our respect for each other grew, and she was learning valuable lessons in a much more powerful and long-lasting way.

At the End of a Pointing Finger

If you've ever had a finger pointed at you, then you know how terrible it feels. To me, it feels like I am naked, and everyone is staring. There is no place to hide, nowhere to run.

When I was about six years old, I had a little friend named Sport. He and I played together often, and one day we decided to throw all the decorative rocks in our neighbor's entrance—a few hundred of them—onto their sidewalk. It never occurred to us that not only was this not our property, but we were essentially vandalizing our neighbor's yard.

Later that day, our neighbor's teenage son came to our door to tell my mom that someone had thrown all their decorative rocks onto the sidewalk. He said that Sport had confessed and indicated it was him and me who did it. There I was, finger pointed squarely at me. My mother asked me in front of my neighbor if this was true. I denied it. In my nakedness, nowhere-to-run-or-hide brain, I decided to lie to get that finger pointed at something, anything, other than me. The result was that Sport had to clean up all of the rocks by himself, and he learned he couldn't count on me. In addition, all the kids in the neighborhood found out that I had lied, which did not help matters.

There are few things worse than knowing you've screwed up and having someone point at you and utter, "What have you done?" It makes you feel small, weak, humiliated, embarrassed, and guilty. Like a dog with his ears down and tail between his legs, we know we did something bad and find it unbearable to have it thrown in our face by others. That is the picture I keep in my mind when my daughter does something impulsive that is dangerous or scary. I remind myself that she already knows it was bad. Pointing a finger at her only increases her negative emotions and it doesn't help her solve her problem. She needs me at her side, supporting her, not sitting across from her pointing fingers.

Judgement = Destruction

Just like finger pointing, passing judgment on ourselves and our children can be incredibly destructive. Being a parent is a tough position, because we are responsible for our child's wellness, but we cannot control their thoughts, behaviors, and emotions. Many of us use judgment as a way to discover the problem.

"What kind of mother would allow her daughter
to cut herself like that?"
"What kind of family lets their kid
miss school because he's depressed?"
"Why doesn't she just enforce the rules
and make her kids follow them?"

These are the kinds of thoughts that make me feel better by pushing others down. Not only is the holier-than-thou feeling fleeting, but I never feel better after I've made these judgmental statements.

That's not to say that all judgments are bad. We need a way to decipher information, and sometimes judgments can be really helpful with that. However, when we are dealing with our friends and family, withholding judgment can actually deepen a relationship, which can, in turn, give us a richer source of information. If I had judged my daughter for looking for attention when she was cutting, then she may not have told me that she had a plan to commit suicide. If our actions, like judging, prevent others from giving us the whole story, then it puts both of us at a disadvantage. For them, it lowers the likelihood that they'll share critical information with others. For us, anything that gets in the way of finding solutions for our daughter's issues means that she suffers longer.

If you happen to have a child or loved one who struggles, then you already know there is plenty of judgment being hurled at them from society as a whole. Your loved ones need more people standing next to them, shoulder to shoulder, instead of looking down their noses at them. For a child, there is nothing more powerful than having a person they can count on, judgment-free.

Acceptance

One of my roles as a mother is that I want to help my kids learn. For my daughter, this means letting her experience some pain points (within reason) and not protecting her from the things life throws at her. So, when she had a conflict with a friend, I decided to let her feel her way through while I served more as the co-pilot on her journey. She was really upset with one friend and simultaneously feeling like a different friend was pulling away from her. While every bone in my body was telling me to fix the situation for her, I held back and let her take the time to discuss all her options.

As we sat in the car, parked on the side of the street after spending time with one friend and on the way to pick up a different one, I asked her questions, reflected what I was hearing, and offered alternatives, much like I might do with one of my clients. It was incredibly difficult, because the critical voice in my head was screaming at me to just tell her the answer and fearing how these girls would perceive my daughter. My ego can be a real jerk. Thankfully, my daughter came to a conclusion about her situation and made a decision about how she wanted to proceed. I reminded her that the possible consequences of her actions may result in a negative response so she could be sure of her actions. She thought for a moment and said, "I really need a break right now, so if my friend decides to be mad about that, then so be it."

I wanted to jump for joy. I wanted to record the moment for posterity. I wanted to tell everyone that my kid already knew what most adults are still trying to learn. And she got there without me fixing, rescuing, or lecturing. I honored her ability to solve her own problems. I accepted her feelings and perceptions and didn't try to argue her out of them or minimize them. In that moment, in that car, she and I had a breakthrough. The walls of defense came down and she felt safe enough to let me see inside her mind.

The gift of acceptance is that it allows us to connect at a deeper level; my daughter was able to let down her guard and be vulnerable with me. I can support my daughter to find her own solutions and I saw a side of my daughter that was filled with wisdom and self-care. She made a decision fully prepared for the fallout. My daughter and I shared a special bond in that car on that street, and it impacted both of us powerfully—all because of the gift of acceptance.

Navigate the Journey

If shame and blame are off the table, and I believe they *need* to be, then what is left?

I believe that the brain is a powerful, complicated, and poorly understood organ. Even neuroscientists acknowledge they've barely scratched the surface of all the workings of this three-pound mass of cells. We have theories, protocols, and anecdotes, but we are far from linking cause to effect. So, when my daughter is not doing well and I am desperate for an answer, when I don't know where to go or what to do, I can remind myself that there is no one answer. If something works today, it might not work tomorrow. If something works for your friend's daughter, it might not work for your daughter. If something does work, a new problem might arise. The complexity of the brain is far beyond our understanding and all we can do is find what works today.

I may want a permanent answer, but I can't necessarily find one. I may search for the right doctor, therapist, treatment, medicine, or residential school, but there isn't a catchall for everything she is experiencing. One program might offer dialectical behavior therapy to manage anxiety and depression, but they don't work with eating disorders. Another place might deal with eating disorders, but they can't work with bipolar kids. Some places focus on addiction rather than mental health. Others focus on integrative medicine and don't deal with pharmaceuticals. There are simultaneously loads of answers and no answers at all.

If the answers are buried in experiences, medicines, therapies, hormonal shifts, nutritional intake, peer groups, and phases of the moon, then we can navigate our way through this maze by paying attention to what we are learning along the way. Keeping logs of moods, side effects, and triggers is helpful. Researching symptoms, causes, and treatments will provide more data to incorporate into the picture. Connecting with support groups of parents going through similar issues can be a great place for camaraderie and advocacy. The shift from finding a single answer to learning more and more about my daughter has me feeling like a PhD researcher studying primates in the wild.

It's a process, so there is no end and no finish line. When I could get that through my thick skull, I felt relief and peace. I could put myself back into my role as mother, advocate, and chief researcher, where my job was to collect and manage the data. More data equals more discoveries. More discoveries lead to better solutions. Better solutions bring longer bouts of stability and wellness and steer away from the judgment, shame, and blame that only serve to pull you off the path to recovery.

Words from Piper

Acceptance
She just wanted to be accepted
How hard can that be?
Her friends they were pretty, skinny, and popular

They wore PINK
They wore makeup, a lot of makeup
They were accepted.
She shaped herself into one of them
The thoughts consumed every part of her
They controlled her.
She turned into them
For what?
To please other people?
Wear what you want
Be who you want to be
Because acceptance is a word that can destroy you
Don't let that be you.

Steps for Moving Forward:

1. When strong emotions arise, try to discern if there is an underlying fear that is driving them. When we become aware of the fear, we can address it.

2. Instead of focusing on finding a single answer, shift your attention to learning. Learning allows children and parents to be on the same side, and it's a far more forgiving approach. The world of mental health is not black and white, so getting used to being in the gray zone is essential.

Exercises:

1. Be vulnerable with your children. Share with them, appropriately, what is going on inside your mind. Vulnerability begets vulnerability, which then promotes connection.

2. Practice mindfulness techniques to engage the parasympathetic (calming center) part of the brain. Calm in the face

of fear and uncertainty allows you to be more approachable for your children during times of high stress and shame.

Section II

Societal Contributors

Chapter 3

Our Kids Are Hurting

To be in your child's memories,
you have to be in their lives today.
–Barbara Johnson

s of 2011, our society has witnessed a huge jump in the
number of children and adolescents with anxiety and
depression. Many professionals in the field of mental
health are calling it an epidemic. Most of us with children are witnessing behaviors that were not common in our generation, and we
are unsure what to do. According to Time magazine, depression
has jumped 37 percent in the past ten years and teen suicides are at
an all-time high. It's also reported that although the rates of mental

illness are rising, there is not a corresponding increase in treatment, meaning our kids are suffering alone and in silence.

To further set the stage, in Dr. Twenge's book *iGen*, she provides a visual representation of how the rates for both male and female teens depression have increased dramatically. It appears exponential after the year 2011.

From a *Psychology Today* article titled "Making iGen's Mental Health Issues Disappear":

> The shift among girls is not a small change—it's a 50% increase. The increase in the suicide rate is also large—according to the CDC, it has tripled among girls and doubled among boys ages 10 to 14 and increased by 50% among 15- to 19-year-olds. In addition, the NS-DUH national screening study found a 50% increase in clinical-level depression among 12- to 17-year-olds in just 4 years (from 2011 to 2015). Another study found that the number of children and teens admitted to hospitals for suicidal thoughts or self-harm doubled over the last 10 years. In other words, the most serious mental health issues showed the largest increases.

Anecdotally and scientifically, we have a generation of children who are struggling. Our kids are hurting.

Anxiety, Anxiety Everywhere

When I talk to teachers and school counselors, they report seeing troubling behaviors that are new since even just ten years ago. Some say that the kids are wound really tight. Others will say there is too much pressure on kids from parents. Still others will say that kids are being inundated with too much technology at a time when they are not developmentally ready to handle the complicated—and sometimes disturbing—input. Theories abound.

We are all looking for what's to blame. We want to find the culprit and put an end to the madness. But much like with finding a single answer to my daughter's emotional angst, life experience tells me it's probably not that easy.

When I ask around about the triggers for anxiety, I receive all kinds of answers. Kids are worried about grades, friends, clothes, weather, car accidents, kidnappers, windowless rooms, being late, being early, body image, college applications, school shootings, athletic competitions, and so much more. When they are in the midst of an anxiety tornado, they struggle to self-regulate and challenge their thoughts. They think in black and white, catastrophize, and set themselves up to not be disappointed. They are simultaneously growing physically, emotionally, intellectually, and spiritually. Their brains are rewiring by the time they get to adolescence, and combined with major changes in their hormone levels, it's easy to imagine the chaos that is the teenage mind.

In a culture of individualism, our children are spending more time discovering who they are and less time connecting with others. It's ironic that in a time when it's possible to connect with anyone, anywhere, anytime, we are all more disconnected than ever. Our kids learn to drive at later ages. They stay home more often than the generations before them. They are less employed and study fewer hours than their parents. They spend an average of four to six hours per day using some type of device to access media online. That means they are seeing more things online in isolation, making them more likely to compare themselves to something that doesn't represent reality and, therefore, feel really bad about themselves. Without anyone else there to challenge their thoughts, they can get lost very quickly.

As their brains rush from thought to thought, it's easy to imagine them going down a rabbit hole, where they aspire to become more popular, smarter, skinnier, prettier, muscular, or more accomplished. They think becoming these things will make them happy, and happy is always the real goal. But happy is fickle and fleeting. Give me a free dessert, and I am happy—for ten minutes. I lose two pounds, and I am happy—for about a day. Get asked out by my secret crush, and I am happy—for about a week. Get an A, and I am happy—until I realize that keeping the A creates a whole world of pressure and stress of its own, and happiness starts to wane. The list goes on and on. All of these external validation schemes are distracting our kids and keeping them running around a track like a pig chasing an Oreo.

When our worthiness depends on the opinions of others, we live in a precarious spot. We may feel like we are falling apart, but we dare not ask for help lest we bring attention to our weaknesses. Nobody wants to be "that kid." So many suffer in silence, and with all the other kids absorbed in their own internal struggles, nobody reaches out to lend a hand. Even if another teen does notice one of their peers struggling, they may choose to ignore or deny it for fear of getting sucked into the drama or being called out by their peer group.

And the adults are struggling too. We all want to help our hurting kids, but we aren't sure what is right, what is useful, and what is appropriate. Teachers are far outnumbered by students, so they can't possibly attend to the throngs of anxious and depressed kids that walk into their classrooms each day. Most schools only have a handful of counselors, psychologists, and social workers, so, again, it's a numbers problem. Parents want to ease their children's suffering, but we feel ill-equipped. Most of us didn't have the level of anxiety that our kids do, and many parents worry their parenting will be called into question if they reach out for help and support.

When we focus on the causes of this anxiety, we take our focus off of what is going on in the moment. If your child broke a leg falling out of a tree, you wouldn't look around for the causes of trees in the neighborhood or what has kids wanting to climb them. You would immediately attend to the pain and try to manage it.

What would happen if we took a similar approach with emotional pain? What would it mean to hear our kids' challenges and attend to them in the moment? What if our kids could share how they feel incredibly stressed and feel pressure to perform, to accomplish, and to be better than someone else? If we accept that our kids are experiencing high levels of anxiety and depression, then we may be able to create a safe space for them to air their concerns and combat the stigma surrounding emotional suffering.

Relationship is Priority #1

Anything that gets in the way of our relationship with our child should be examined intensely. As a parent whose anxiety, shame, and fear gets between myself and my kids, I know the pattern all too well. Forming deep and meaningful relationships with our children and teens can help them weather their storms, of which there will be many, more smoothly and without questioning their worth or lovable-ness.

A wise therapist once told me to never put grades above my relationship with my son. When she said it, I realized that it never occurred to me that I have to cultivate and nurture my relationship with my son. I just assumed that I was his mom, and so it would be, forever and always. It seems obvious now, but I really didn't work on my connection with him. I was too busy floundering around trying to do everything right and using his behavior as my yardstick.

For instance, if he got an A, then I was a good mom. If he kicked a goal, I was a good mom. If he weighed the right weight and grew to the right height, then I was a good mom. Imagine how my core was shaken when he got an in-school suspension, or a C, or missed a basketball shot. He felt my disappointment, and I felt ashamed for being so attached to his performance.

When I began to focus on our relationship, I could breathe again. His grades were his, and I could provide support and guidance, but I wasn't attached to them in a way that created distance between us. If he got an A, then he did it himself and could feel the full force of pride and excitement. If he got a D+, which he did one semester in Honors English, then he felt the full force of missing an important essay and will remember that feeling as he begins his next semester. Either way, we are in partnership together, working towards his successes. When he falls, he picks himself back up and we discuss what happened and what he learned, same as when he does a great job.

For my daughter, this perspective has been absolutely pivotal for her mental health and wellness. As she struggles to cope with her intense emotions, I can be on her team, supporting and standing by her every step of the way. When she is feeling suicidal, she can tell me. Our relationship is strong and my love unconditional. She doesn't fear repercussions. Instead, she wants me to be with her in the fear and the emotional roller coaster. When she is out of control, I am a touchstone for her. There is no need to hide, since we accept each other fully as we are.

My daughter has found it difficult to make and keep friends. Some kids don't understand what it means when she has to go to the hospital. Others tell her that their parents don't want them hanging around her because of her illness (seriously!). Still others try to foster a friendship with her only to find it impossible when she becomes anxious or depressed and pushes them away. These kids are still in middle school, so I don't expect them to be able to understand and handle the ups and downs of her emotional roller coaster. However, I am happy to report that she has found some nice girls who refuse to give up on her. They seem to recognize unconditional love. When they stand by her regardless of her behavior, my heart swells and I find hope that she will be able to connect with others too.

Let Teens Lead

When I force myself to step back and ask my kids for their ideas, I am usually stunned by what they have to say. In my many attempts to control that which is out of my control, I have discovered that kids can think well and come up with creative solutions on their own. If you have ever done the timed marshmallow tower challenge where you are tasked with building the tallest structure with dry spaghetti noodles, tape, and string upon which a marshmallow is placed, then you know it is kindergarteners who scored third after engineers and CEO's. Because our kids haven't been indoctrinated into the "boxes" that adults tend to put ourselves in, they can come up with some ingenious and unique approaches.

As an adult, I often put myself in the box of having to be in charge, know the answer, and assume all responsibility. Many of my adult peers do this as well. Take a peak in any school and you will likely see an environment where the adult is standing in the front of the room, talking or lecturing, and providing information to the children. The typical model is for adults to lead and kids to follow. But what if we empowered students to create a system of support for each other? What ideas might they try?

My daughter has asked me to step back, stop fixing, and give up the lecturing. She has shared with me that, most of the time, she just needs me to hear what she is saying without judgment. When I can do this for her, I find that she comes up with some terrific plans to overcome her own challenges. For example, she has a whole nightly routine that she's developed to help her get ready for bed. She gives me her phone at eight o'clock, then starts a shower or bath, turns on her diffuser, prepares her school work for the next day, lowers her lights, and snuggles with her guinea pigs. This allows her to see if her anxiety fires up and if she needs to tweak her system. When it's her own plan, she is obviously more invested in it, making the plan more sustainable over time.

In a world where stability is the name of the game, long-term, healthy behaviors are critical. Many of you might be thinking about what to do with behaviors that are probably detrimental to her mental health. Well, it's the same game.

For example, I believe that social media is too advanced, nuanced, and subtle for young teens to comprehend, as they are not developmentally ready to manage and notice the dopamine surges they receive as a result of using many apps, pages, and sites. My daughter's anxiety and self-image were being triggered by posts she was receiving on different social media outlets. Each time she would go into a free fall after reading something or seeing a photo, I would have to bite my tongue to stop myself from saying, "I told you so."

On her third hospitalization discharge, I asked the psychiatrist and social worker what they see social media doing to most kids who come to the hospital. They were frank and replied that social media isn't good for kids, especially those with mental illness. They asked my daughter if she would consider not using it, and she weakly agreed. Then they asked her how long she could commit to staying off social media, and she said a few days. So, they encouraged her to agree to one month, and she acquiesced. Once she was home and off social media for several weeks, she told me that she realized how addictive it was for her and that she doesn't really want to be on it anymore. By letting her take the lead, she came to the realization on her own without me harping at her and potentially damaging our relationship in the process.

When there needs to be a hard "no" to something, like having a cell phone after eight o'clock, then I do that too (more on parenting needing to continue later). I simply try to minimize the controls I have to put in place and instead encourage her to make them and enforce them herself.

We all parent differently, and we all have our own values and beliefs that will guide how we decide to run things at home. I think parenting is tough enough without judging each other harshly. I also think we can model compassion and love with each other, and we can show our kids how to treat each other kindly because, need I remind you, our kids are hurting.

I have found that our daughter must learn what does and does not work on her own. She is far too stubborn to take my word for it, and she truly learns best through experiencing things herself. If I believe that something is truly dangerous to her well-being, then I do intervene, such as locking up medications and sharp objects. But when there are lessons to learn when things might be painful, but not life-threatening, that is where I draw the fine line. My daughter knows this and will typically agree. Allowing her to determine what to control in her world has helped her bump into lots of challenges, and as she weaves her way through them, she learns where she can and cannot go. I view my job as walking next to her, supporting her, and loving her through these discoveries, only intervening when necessary.

Our Kids Are Watching

Be the change you want to see in the world.
–Ghandi

Dr. Brene Brown, one of my heroes and author of *Daring Greatly*, says that kids are more likely to notice what we do than what we say. So, if we want kids who are compassionate and open to connecting with all sorts of people, then we probably need to do that ourselves. Developing our own self-awareness and self-care shows our kids how to also so those things and sets the foundation by which they can emerge into a healthy relationship with themselves and others.

The other day, my daughter and I were coming out of the gym and a man approached us. It was really cold out and he was dressed shabbily. He asked me if I had any money that I could spare so he could get breakfast. I immediately pulled out $10 and handed it to him. As soon as he walked away, my daughter turned to me and said, "Good job, Mom!"

She was watching. She saw me look at a stranger with love and generosity without any judgment of who he was or what he needed. He asked. I provided. She witnessed.

Even as I spend time writing this book, I wonder if my kids think I spend too much time working. Am I on my phone too much? Am I distracted by social media? Do I spend enough time with them? Do they feel loved and worthy? I've found it useful to ask my kids how they are feeling about our time together, if they can share any special memories of us, or if they can come up with a family mantra. Another useful source of feedback is having the other adults in their lives share how our kids speak about us when we aren't in the room.

Now, when I speak, I am more aware of the language I use, what I choose to share, and the judgments and opinions I might be presenting. If I allow myself to scoff at a parent whose child is having a tantrum, then I am showing my kids that I have no compassion. If I remark on somebody's body size or appearance, then they learn that our worthiness comes from how we look. If I tolerate bad behavior by them or others, then I am setting them up to do the same. Being a parent is more than just raising a child, which is already huge endeavor. It's also being the person I want them to be, which means developing and growing myself.

As our kids reveal that they are hurting, isolated, and disconnected, I want for us to create a world where they can communicate their fears and struggles without fear of being judged. Because our kids are watching us, we have a golden opportunity to show them how this is done. We can model making mistakes, exposing our fears, and feeling our feelings. They can see us offer compassion, love, and understanding to those around us. They can hear the words we use and mimic the language of kindness and openness. Most importantly, they can experience the safety and comfort of being loved unconditionally, which they can translate into their own relationships, and perhaps help each other hurt a little less.

Words From Piper
I Cried Out
Why?
Why me?
Why am I such a failure?
Why is everyone giving up on me?
Why is this happening?
Finally I just gave up on myself
I didn't care what was going to happen to me
I didn't matter anymore
They threw me out like a piece of trash
But that's how life works, right?
Some people won't care enough to care for you
Some people will throw you out
But in the end, if they give up on you they weren't worth it
in the first place.

Run
I want to run away
To a place I can be free
A place I can feel loved
A place where I matter for once
A place where I can find my peace
Why can't I go to that place?
Why do I have to feel like this?
Every second of everyday
Lonely
Worthless
Helpless
Unlovable

It's ok though
Because someday I'll find that place
That place I can be happy for the first time
The place I have meaning in
Hopefully.

Lost

I was lost
No place felt like home
I had no one to go to
I had lost myself
I had lost my hope
I lost everything
But that's life
Right?
You get thrown around
You get walked all over
You get played
This life is full of bad times
I never guessed it would happen to me

Happy

As I step on the scale
The number higher than I expected
Why?
Why am I so fat?
Every time the number goes up the lower I go
Dinner time comes
Fear running through my mind
What do I do?

The answer is simple
Don't eat
Don't drink
Don't keep anything down
The number will drop
I'll be happy then
Won't I?

Steps for Moving Forward:

1. Look at the data. Each community is different, so becoming familiar with the struggles in your area can help you to get familiar with what your children are facing.
2. Put your relationship with your child above their performance. By nurturing your connection with them, you are setting yourself up to weather storms with them and have them coming to you for support and guidance.
3. Include your children in creating solutions. Let them experiment so they can learn what works, that failure is helpful and nothing to be ashamed of, and how to recover from setbacks.

Exercises:

1. Try a natural consequences approach. When they are making a decision that you think is not a good choice, try letting them do it anyway (caveat: unless it's dangerous!). My favorite example is letting my son go to the bus stop without a hat and gloves in the winter. When I let him experience the consequence of being uncomfortably cold, he learns to tweak his decision next time.
2. Try modeling the characteristics and values you want your children to have. Lecturing not allowed!

Chapter 4

Let's Raise Compassionate Kids

Most parents acknowledge that it's impossible for a handful of school counselors with over 1,000 students to meet the rapidly increasing mental health needs of the students. For example, in our local high schools, we have about four counselors for roughly 1,500 students. Let's say we double the number of counselors. That still would have each counselor responsible for about 200 kids.

It seems like it would be more effective to teach our kids how to care for each other. You don't have to have a degree in psychology to have empathy for another person. If we can teach our kids how to care for and support each other in healthy ways, and we can model that behavior for them, then our kids can be trained to take action and help alleviate pain for one another.

Middle School Madness

When I ask people about their middle school experiences, they typically stiffen up, take a deep breath, and respond with negative comments. Middle school seems to be an island of misfits where kids tear each other up. Developmentally, we know that middle schoolers are becoming more independent, concerned about their peers, and aware of themselves. They are looking for belonging, and, unfortunately, they are trying to fit in by excluding others. To add insult to injury, these kids went from an environment of high stability in elementary school with a single teacher for a majority of their school day to one of instability with six to eight teachers per day. It is difficult for the kids to connect with any one teacher, and difficult for the teacher to connect with any one of a hundred or so kids. At a time when our kids would greatly benefit from the wisdom and guidance of a caring adult, we throw them a curve ball by reducing their opportunities to form strong relationships with any adults.

My stepmother is a retired principal with over forty years of experience. If she were ruler for one day, she would have middle school teachers teach multiple subjects per day, like elementary teachers, so that kids would have a higher probability of connecting with their teachers. Her theory is that because the kids and teachers in middle school have a low likelihood of attaching deeply, there is no adult in a leadership role and kids are forced to take control. And when middle schoolers take control, they tend to do it through power moves like bullying, coercing, and excluding. By increasing the time kids spend with one teacher and decreasing the number of children the teacher must manage throughout the day, adults could take back the leadership roles in the building. I might be biased, but I really like this idea.

When I walk through the halls of any middle school, I see adolescents who are constantly looking around to see who is looking at them. It's a time when their peers' opinions matter greatly. They are desperate to fit in, and the stress is visible in their faces, the way they carry themselves, and how they speak about themselves and others. As they are trying to figure out who they are, they are falling into the trap of fearing how they will be judged. Instead of experiencing meaningful self-awareness, they are comparing themselves to others and finding that they don't measure up (which of course is a common result of comparison). It's a game that can't be won.

If our kids felt safe to expose who they are, experiment with different personas, and give each other a wide berth, I can't help but wonder what they would find. Instead of expending all their energy hiding who they are and contorting themselves to fit in, they might become curious, open-minded, and supportive of each other.

Imagine a middle school where kids took care of each other rather than rip each other apart. While I don't know for sure the impact that environment would have, I strongly believe it would be exponentially superior to the one that currently exists for our young teens.

Cultural Mores

We were at our daughter's dietician appointment the other day, and the dietician looked right into my daughter's eyes and advised her not to look at magazines or watch shows created in Hollywood. This dietician has over thirty years of experience working with girls who suffer from eating disorders. She told my daughter that the girls and women in those venues are mostly sick and unhealthy. In our country, we have glamorized a dangerous and, for the most part, unattainable vision of beauty for females. As our adolescent girls begin to explore who they are, they are bumping up against our unnatural cultural standards. They are dancing between being a girl and being a woman, being naïve and being sexy, being playful and being seductive, being comfortable with their bodies and being ashamed for having body fat or small breasts or large thighs or thin lips. When we showcase women who use their bodies to gain attention, power, and control, we are teaching our girls that the way they look is their most important attribute.

Because the way we look continues to change over our life-times, it seems like we are handing our girls a raw deal. There is one guarantee about our looks: the body will age. It's a battle that cannot be won, so why would we send our girls into such an arena? To make matters worse, we are preparing our girls to measure their worthiness by external validation. It's a double whammy. They are being shown that inevitable aging is the enemy *and* that they are only as good as they look, which is measured against an impossible yardstick.

Let's set aside the body image issues we have in our culture for a moment and take a peek into our expectations for girls. At young ages, we see girls believing they can do and be anything. But by the time they hit middle school, girls begin to see them-selves in more traditional female roles. We know the percentage of girls in science- and math-oriented activities and classes is much lower than their male counterparts. They don't self-report as being able to become president or CEO someday, even if it's something they want. In the US, we still have a significant wage gap between males and females. We see few women in positions of high business acumen, political office, or even humanitarian efforts.

As a woman who spent over twenty years in a man's world as a chemical engineer in the oil industry, I can personally vouch for the way women are treated in this country in male-dominated fields. It wasn't a given that I could do the job, had the training, and was intellectually capable. I had to prove myself over and over again, while I watched my male colleagues not being put under the same scrutiny.

Of course, some of this was caused by my own hang ups, and I was desperate to fit in, so I was more than willing to tolerate bad behavior in order to show I was part of the club. I want for all women to be able to do their jobs without second guessing themselves simply because of their gender, and I want our girls to observe this on a regular basis.

Now I'm raising a daughter who is entering the world of figuring out who she is. I want her to continue to care for others, be her highly empathic self, and be comfortable in her own skin. Is it really necessary for her to be kicked around psychologically and emotionally by our culture? Our cultural standards are hindering her growth and have her hiding her true self. While many of our greatest lessons are learned through difficulty and struggle, I want to make a clear distinction between struggle and cruelty. When we give our girls *impossible* goals, shame them for having a body without a thigh gap, and show them a world where women are not valued for their thoughts and intellect, I would call that pretty darn cruel.

The Beds are All Full

Not only is there a shortage of school support for kids who are struggling, but the mental health field is finding that demand is far exceeding supply. During our first visit to the ER for our daughter's suicidal ideation, we were surprised to find that child and adolescent mental health is not covered at most hospitals. In fact, there are only a few facilities that work with kids in our state. Therefore, we were asked to wait in the ER while they called around to see if there were any beds available. After six hours of waiting, I was given instructions to deliver our daughter to a facility about two hours away. Imagine my surprise when we arrived at this facility only to find that they did not actually have a bed for her, and they directed me to another facility an hour away.

We arrived there at two o'clock in the morning, had her admitted by four o'clock, and I was finally back home by six o'clock. Being awake for twenty-four hours and carting my unstable child all over creation really put the state of children's mental health care into perspective for me: it's a mess.

In a nutshell, there aren't enough providers, treatment programs, and mental health hospitals to address the needs of our kids. Psychiatrists are booking three months in advance. Day treatment programs have long waiting lists. Most therapists will take weeks or months for an initial consult. The emergency room is the first line of defense for a suicidal child, where there may not be a child psychiatrist on staff. In addition to not being able to stay in the same hospital as the ER, a child has to wait until a child psychiatrist can be contacted and called in to perform a videoconference or telephone consult which will determine the child's fate. It's just so darn inefficient.

If our kids have higher rates of mental illness and access to the care and support needed to recover is severely restricted, then our kids will have to either wait or go without help. This seems unreasonable and unfair, especially as a parent watching your child suffer. Our children are experiencing a lack of resources in their schools and their communities, but if our children can develop the skills and mindsets to take care of each other, it would unload some of the burden from systems that are understaffed and underprepared for the increase in demand.

Fear and Judgment

As if limited resources weren't a big enough hurdle for our kids to overcome, we also have to address the stigma associated with mental illness. Those who suffer may hide their illness. Parents may not want anyone to know. Their friends may not know what to do or say, so they stay away. Teachers who don't understand how to handle certain brain disorders may worry about doing the wrong thing and inadvertently alienate certain children. As I've learned from personal experience, parents may even advise their own children to stay away from a child with mental illness out of fear and ignorance. The world of mental illness is a pretty judgmental place, which doesn't serve anyone well.

When our daughter began cutting, she was treated like a pariah. The school asked her to cover her arms for fear that other kids would copy her. Parents of her friends forbade their kids from hanging out with our daughter for fear that cutting was contagious. The lunch room staff tried to separate the kids who were "cutters" and told them to stop hanging out with each other for fear that these kids would have undue negative influence on others and themselves. I was even asked to join my daughter on a field trip because the teacher feared not knowing what to do if my daughter became anxious.

Fear swarms around kids who have emotional struggles and disorders in the way they think and process information. It's natural to fear what we don't understand. However, this type of exclusionary treatment only exacerbates the issues these kids are facing, and it teaches the rest of the kids that it's okay to ignore or shut out certain people in life, like those who struggle with mental health.

When I think about how we lock up the mentally ill and keep them hidden from society in hospitals and facilities, I wonder if there is a better way. Kids who suffer mental health issues are hard-pressed to befriend and socialize with "normal" kids. It seems a shame that even though a healthy child can be a real attribute and model for a kid with distorted thinking, we don't allow or encourage the two groups to cross-pollinate very much. If we are indeed the average of the five people with whom we spend the most time, as research has shown, then each mentally ill kid would benefit from having a few mentally healthy kids to add to their group. The healthy kids are kept away from mentally ill ones, and the mentally ill kids are kept away from the healthy ones. At a time when peers have such a huge influence, it would make more sense to pair kids with different strengths so they can show each other how to navigate life and embrace a different perspective than their own.

Me, Myself, and I

Our culture rewards and encourages individuality. Each generation is more self-focused than the one before it. Today's young people don't participate in communal activities where they depend on and take care of each other. They don't go to churches, they don't get married, they drive alone, and they post a plethora of selfies. The focus is on fierce independence, which has both its benefits and drawbacks.

From the perspective of our children, the dark side of individuality is never asking for help, not extending a hand to help others, and feeling isolated, misunderstood, and disconnected. Sure, self-sufficiency is important. But there is a cost when it is prioritized above compassion.

If we teach our kids to take care of themselves to the exclusion of taking care of others, the result is having no one to go to when they have a problem. As a self-proclaimed "compassionator," I can attest to the risks of caring for others and not myself. Bu when I learned that I could support others without fixing, saving, rescuing, and enabling them, my whole world opened up. I could exercise my empathy without getting sucked into the drama or losing myself in the mix. When I can show compassion without fear of getting screwed or betrayed or used, I can use it all the time. Another added bonus is that I can show compassion to myself, which is a much nicer way to live.

Our daughter had an incident in seventh grade that is a great example of how our society teaches our kids to mind their own business. She had a friend who was really struggling with some issues around sexuality. Because her friend is from a devoutly religious home that forbids homosexuality, she was hiding her thoughts and feelings, which resulted in a very stressful existence. One day during class, my daughter's friend suddenly got up from her desk and ran from the room in tears. My daughter said she stared at the teacher to see what she would do. Unfortunately, the teacher did nothing. She didn't address the student who bolted from the class, nor did she speak to the students and ask someone to go check on her. My daughter swims in empathy and compassion, and she could not stand the thought of her friend being left to deal with her pain all alone.

My daughter made the decision to do something. She asked her teacher if she could return a book to the library. Her teacher agreed and my daughter did comply. She also stopped by the bathroom on her way back to class to check on her friend. She found her friend crying and spiraling out of control. My daughter sat with her until she calmed down, and then my daughter returned to class. She told the teacher that she took so long because she had checked on her friend and then returned to her seat.

Not only did the teacher not ask about my daughter's friend who was clearly upset and having a problem, but she contacted the dean of students to give my daughter an in-school lunch detention for lying about where she was going. When the dean called me later that day to share what happened, I asked, "What should my daughter do when she sees a student who is hurting and the adults in the building appear to be doing nothing to lend a hand?"

The dean responded that my daughter should worry about herself and trust that the teacher has it under control. Without any feedback or information being offered to the students, my daughter isn't convinced that anyone in the school is caring about kids. What she witnesses instead is a student bolting from class in tears and the teacher doing nothing. It seems we are asking her to blindly trust, which is not what we want our kids to do. We want her to question, be curious, and observe the world. We want her to develop her critical thinking skills. We want her to be healthily skeptical and use her own instincts. To her, there is a huge discrepancy between what she is being told and what she is seeing with her own eyes on a daily basis.

It broke my heart to hear the dean tell me to instruct my daughter to mind her own beeswax. As our kids are experiencing unprecedented levels of anxiety and depression, it is difficult to believe that the adults have matters under control. If our drive to be self-sufficient has gone a little too far, then perhaps it's time to take a step back. A small step might be allowing kids to check on a friend who runs from a classroom in tears. Another might be to teach our kids how to help each other without becoming enmeshed in another's dilemma. Yet another might be to recognize and reward students who help someone else, especially when both kids became better as a result.

Of course, one anecdote does not a trend make. But the above is just one of many stories. If we can at least agree that our culture places a high value on individualism, then we can start the conversation about the pros and cons. Rather than seeing a black and white issue where kids are either totally self-absorbed or completely selfless creatures, we can begin nudging ourselves towards setting up an environment for our kids to develop empathy and compassion in healthy ways, so they can, in turn, help one another.

Words From Piper

Clay
She wakes up in the morning
Scars on her wrists
Blades lay there on her bed
But you wouldn't know that
She goes down the rigid stairs to get some clay
She picks out her perfect skin tone color and goes back up the staircase
With her blade she slowly cuts out a beautiful smile, welcoming and warm.
Then some vibrant blue eyes, happy and calm
She adds on a nice slim nose, pretty and skinny
Perfect
Now you won't have to ask her if she's okay

You won't have her gray dull eyes and her depressed frown
You won't know how numb she is on the inside
You won't see how emotionally drained she is
You won't know any of that
Because the clay can hide everything
Just like a smile can hide a million feelings
So think next time you see someone put on a smile you never know what lies beneath it.

Steps for Moving Forward:

1. Learn how to care for others without fixing them and model that behavior for your child. Most people want to be heard and acknowledged, which means you can simply listen to them and validate how they are feeling. Less talking on your end is better.

2. Model compassion for yourself so your children can learn to be nice to themselves. We all have voices in our minds that criticize us, tell us mean things, and have us believe we aren't good enough. By showing your children how to manage those voices and understand the role they play, our kids can learn to quiet the negative voices and hear the positive ones more often.

Exercises:

1. Try detaching, which is caring for someone without fixing them. This may look like listening to your children without fixing their problem. Instead, ask a "what" or "how" question to help them develop their own answer, share a personal story of your own with them, or simply pull out the emotion they are exhibiting and reflect that back to them.

2. Try a "should" ban. The word "should" is loaded with judgment and criticism, so try going one week without using this word. Notice how your compassion meter starts to rise when you stop "shoulding" on yourself and others. If this ban is done as a family, then you can share what you are learning together.

Chapter 5

Social Media Is a Real Problem

When I was a young kid, I remember my grandma lamenting that the problem with society was denim jeans. She thought that jeans were for manual laborers. When everyone started wearing them, it brought down the quality of a community.

Just like my grandma, I feel like social media is harming our society, especially our kids' daily lives. It seems to me that social media has taken all means of truly connecting and belonging and thrown them out the window. Instead of building kids up, social media tears them down. If our kids are not developmentally able to distinguish between reality and the fake world created online, then social media is abusive to their growing brains.

Comparison

When I think about social media, I mostly consider how it encourages us to compare ourselves to others. Comparison itself is not the problem, as I see it. Instead, it's when we determine our own worth based on something we *think* is real in another person. For example, when I see a post of a lovely family of four on an exotic vacation, sporting gorgeous tans and perfect smiles, my ego wakes up and clobbers me with comparing my family to theirs. Instead of being happy for them for enjoying a beautiful getaway, I make all sorts of assumptions about them. They must smile and love each other all the time. Look at how great they all look. Their teeth are perfect. They must have oodles of money and free time to be able to take a vacation like that. They probably have no problems at all.

If my ego is really fired up, I might proceed to look in the mirror. I can focus on my painfully pale skin. I can notice my teeth are not perfectly white and aligned. I can focus on the amount of time my kids spend in their room and on their phones instead of laughing and hugging each other. I can feel sad that we don't have any photos of our family in Fiji. I can get resentful that we don't have enough money to travel like them and let out a big, long sigh.

I'm a forty-four-year-old woman who has the life experience to know better, yet I still get caught up in the unhealthy comparison game. Now, consider what this does to an adolescent. I can't imagine the pressure they must feel when they see a photo of their peers doing something they might want to do. I've watched my daughter emulate sexy looks, provocative dancing, dangerous eating habits, rude language, and even different methods of suicide. Our adolescents are already preprogrammed to use their peers as guides to what is and is not acceptable. Unfortunately, their peers are posting things online that don't just raise eyebrows, but are downright unhealthy, dangerous, and sometimes life-shattering.

The adolescent developmental stage has them considering their peers more often, which is closely related to comparing themselves to others. In middle school, kids start to break away from the influence of their parents and move towards the influence of their friends. They become keenly aware of the people around them and concerned with how they are being perceived and judged. It's a difficult time, since they are simultaneously trying to figure out who they are. Being preoccupied with other's perceptions of them makes this journey difficult, because the conditions don't support experimentation, taking risks, and trying on different personas. The risk of getting it wrong is high, and many kids fear being excluded if they don't fit in and use comparison as their guide.

When our daughter was in the depths of her depression, she developed a coping skill around her eating. She would both restrict calories and binge and purge. She became completely disgusted with her body—and thereby disgusted with herself—when she would eat food. Her troubling eating pattern was so bad that during one hospitalization a feeding tube was inserted for several days to provide her body with nourishment.

After that particular hospitalization, I looked through her laptop and phone and found searches for "acceptable body weight," "BMI," "anorexic diets," "how to get a thigh gap," and "how to lose weight quickly." She had looked at photo after photo of unhealthy, thin girls taking selfies of their ribs, hip bones, and collar bones. With direct access to this type of information, my daughter was able to fully immerse herself into a dark world of suffering.

I do not blame online media for the rise in teens struggling with emotional stresses, but I do think it is a negative contributor. While developmentally I have the maturity and self-control to not look at certain types of sites online, my children do not. While I know that negative information and images make me feel negatively, my kids do not. While I know that I am the result of how I spend my time and with whom, my kids do not. Online media is not inherently evil, but it is the gateway to information that can be detrimental to the growth and development of our kids.

Swipe Left

The world of online media is riddled with calls to action. We swipe right for the prettier face, swipe left for the sexier body. Our news feeds lure us to click. Many of our social media sites are designed to advertise and market directly to us. Online media is designed to be incredibly appealing to each individual person, and they can keep upping the ante when we perform tasks or searches showing them what we like and don't like.

The message our kids are getting is that they are only as worthy as the number of 'likes' or hearts or follows or com-ments they receive. There is a direct correlation between how my daughter is treated online and how she feels about herself. When she posts a video and receives lots of praise, she feels worthy, popular, and influential. When she receives a negative comment, she crumbles into a heap of self-hatred, sadness, and depression.

As a parent, I want my daughter to know that she is worthy of love and belonging, regardless of anything someone else says or does. I remind her of this on a regular basis. I talk to her about the blessings she has in her life. I shower her with unconditional love.

But I am learning that I cannot compete with the depth and breadth of the messages she is receiving from online media.

Just like my grandma wouldn't allow me to wear jeans, my own mother suggests that we take smartphones away from kids. I've certainly considered it. We tried banning all online activity for months, and I have to admit that it had mixed results. Without practicing how to interact in a healthy manner with online media, my daughter wasn't able to develop the skills of knowing which types of sites or information were safe or healthy for her. She might be easily upset by certain kinds of posts that my son wouldn't think twice about. Therefore, I think the goal is to navigate online media *with* our kids, which has the inherent goal of also creating deep and meaningful relationships with them. If we can help them grow into an adult who can decipher between positive and negative uses of online media, as well as having the skills to think about long-term consequences, taking away all smartphones doesn't seem like the way to get there.

My daughter's access to online media is severely limited, but I am not naïve. I know that she can find ways around my rules, so limiting her access alone isn't enough. I do follow her online and make sure she is posting appropriate material, but even that isn't terribly effective since I can't follow her around the clock.

I have allowed her to make mistakes online before and suffer some of the consequences of her actions, but sometimes she struggles to recover, and that's a dangerous risk for her. The additional issue is that all of her friends have mostly unlimited access. They all have multiple social media accounts. They can use their phones and laptops in their rooms away from prying eyes. She lives in a world where there are very few hurdles to gaining access to information. Again, this is why we shifted the goal to practicing appropriate online behavior rather than attempting to remove technology completely.

It's Not Real

The image we put online is meant to impress others. For example, I don't post comments about my daughter's suicide attempt or my son's poor grade in English. I don't talk about how my house hasn't been thoroughly cleaned in about six months because I spend every moment of my life trying to keep my head above water trying to get my daughter the resources she needs, while simultaneously trying to connect with my son and husband, as well as run a small business. I don't show photos of the cellulite on my thighs, the bags under my eyes, or the extra chin that sometimes pops up in the wrong lighting. This means that the persona I have created online is not accurate and my eyelashes in my head shot are falsies. Therefore, I would suggest that you not make assumptions about me, my life, my family, my beauty, my financial situation, my parenting, or my business prowess based on what you see about me online—or anyone else for that matter. If you are older than eighteen, you might be able to do that. If not, it's probably a lot tougher.

In the midst of one of my daughter's dark spells, she said that she had no friends. So, she decided that she was going to lose a bunch of weight so that people would like her. I asked her to help me understand how her weight could be connected to her friendships. She assured me that weight was a huge predictor of friendships, and then she proceeded to show me the posts of the girls she perceived to have *all* the friends. To her credit, these young ladies were all terribly thin, wore a lot of makeup, and dressed provocatively. To my daughter's thirteen-year-old mind, she assumed that people liked these girls because of their looks, and so it made sense that she could gain popularity by looking like them.

When I challenged my daughter's assumptions about these girls, she remarked that these girls are perfect. They get good grades in school. Their families are awesome. They don't have any issues with confidence or self-esteem. They never worry that they aren't good enough. They make all the sports teams because they are naturally athletic.

It's easy to see how an adolescent's assumptions can quickly run amok. If someone is popular, then suddenly they are perfect and everything in their lives comes easily. It's a pretty slippery slope, wouldn't you agree?

One particular girl that my daughter thinks has an easy life appears to me as an unhappy and insecure young lady. I suspect she doesn't eat enough calories and appears to be twenty to thirty pounds underweight. She has poor posture and walks with her shoulders rolled forward. She rarely smiles and is constantly looking around to see who is looking at her. When I mentioned these things to my daughter, she said that I was wrong. She couldn't entertain the possibility that this girl had any difficulties or deficiencies. She refused to accept that everyone has flaws and issues, even the popular girls. Teens are known for their distorted thinking, and that thinking seems to be even more pronounced in our daughter, as with many teens struggling with mental illness.

One of the problems with online media is that what is shown is not always real. Being able to distinguish between what is real and what is fake takes practice and experience, as well as a certain level of brain development. The reason I, a middle-aged woman, know that nobody is perfect comes from meeting loads of people who I assumed had easy lives and discovering that they have struggles too. It isn't realistic for my daughter to meet all the people she sees online, so it will be more difficult for her to challenge her biased beliefs. Also, when I can connect with people in an authentic manner, we share all the parts of ourselves. If our kids don't feel safe to connect with each other authentically for fear of someone posting about them online, especially during their middle school years when peers matter so much, they won't be able to connect deeply and discover each other's strengths *and* weaknesses. The line between reality and fantasy is blurred with online media as their main lens, so our kids have trouble learning what is real and what is not.

Pressure Cooker

Online media is just another way for kids to communicate information to the world. Because online media is open to the world and anyone can access it, it can be hard to defend yourself. In social situations, and even on the phone, we can create boundaries to escape from others' bad behavior. Those boundaries don't exist in the world of online media. Because our kids have little recourse to comments or attacks on them made online, they worry about the fallout: who will read it, what their peers will think, and how to handle it.

At a time in their lives when their peer's perceptions are most important, online media has kids feeling like they are sitting in a pressure cooker. Our kids don't know what to post, what others will post, when things will be posted, whether or not certain things will be posted, who will see their posts, etc. The number of unknowns is sky high, and it adds tremendous amounts of stress to their lives.

For example, there was a group of kids from a local middle school who started an online media account where they would post "roasts" of other kids. For those of us who are older, we might think of roasting as poking fun at others in good jest. For our kids, roasting is posting something negative about a person where anyone and everyone can see it. They posted about a girl in their class being a stalker and made fun of her for copying the popular girls. They publicly shamed her, what she wore, how she looked and behaved. This type of exchange hurts the kids who post the negative information, the kid who is being posted about, and the kids who are reading the exchanges. Nobody wins in this scenario.

There was another incident where a middle school girl was being picked on by a group of her peers. After months of being tormented by them, she posted on a shared media site that she wanted to physically hurt the girls who were picking on her. When my daughter showed me the post, I found the message alarming. However, instead of seeing a girl who was aggressive and dangerous, I saw an adolescent who was stressed out, under a lot of pressure, and begging for help.

Unfortunately, she did not receive help and support from the school and was suspended for her threat to do bodily harm to the group of girls who were bullying her. The kids who picked on this girl learned that pushing someone to the edge is acceptable. The girl who was suspended learned that nobody is going to protect or support her. The kids who witnessed the whole scenario learned that even if you are being antagonized, you'd better keep your mouth shut or you'll get in more trouble. Is this what we would ever deliberately teach kids? I think not.

There is a video titled "Justice Monkey" on YouTube, and it shows an experiment where two capuchin monkeys perform a task and each monkey is given a slice of cucumber as a result. In the video, the researchers suddenly give one monkey a grape and the other a slice of cucumber to see if they take issue with the inequity of the reward, where the new reward of grapes is better than the repeated cucumber. The monkey who received the cucumber proceeds to toss the cucumber at the researcher after watching her fellow monkey get a grape and grab the cage bars in anger, shaking them with her little monkey fists. The conclusion is that even monkeys can indeed discern injustice, and they react accordingly.

I keep this image of the angry monkey in my mind when I think about teenage brains. Our kids know injustice. They know what it looks like and what it feels like. They can sense it when it happens to them and to others.

When I think about the injustices our children witness frequently on social media, I wonder how it impacts their thoughts, their brains, and their development. How many injustices can a human brain tolerate before they begin to impact someone's sense of emotional well-being? What happens when our kids see hundreds of injustices fly under the radar in a single week? What happens when we desensitize our evolutionary need for justice to form tribes for safety and survival? Data shows that our kids are experiencing higher levels of emotional issues, and I can't help but think that social media is part of the reason.

Constant, Incessant, and Non-Stop

For most adults, these problems with adolescents and teens are nothing new. We all remember being the outcast or being bullied and excluded. The big difference between then and now is that technology provides a pipeline that makes it easier to behave badly. Social media is constant, incessant, and non-stop. Just watch today's adolescents and teens and notice how often they look at their phones. For many, there is no downtime, no respite.

When I was a kid, I could escape the social drama at school. When I went home, I was safe from further attacks, comments, inside jokes, condescending stares, and giggles that I was sure were aimed at me. In that safe place, I could process what had happened. I could experience the range of emotions and then come to conclusions. I could work through what I wanted to do the next day, make a plan, and move on. In short, I had time. Online media is always available, which doesn't allow our kids to take the time to slow down, think things through, process their emotions, and then move on.

In addition, social media is designed to be addicting. We know that our brain gets little shots of dopamine when we see that someone looked at our post, "liked" our photo, or posted a comment on our chat. Dopamine feels good, so we want it and will seek those things that ensure its release. We are literally pulled towards social media by our brains, so it is no surprise that many of us, including our kids, feel and behave as though we cannot live without it.

The insidious part of online media is that it's a constant dial of whether someone is "in" or "out." The gauge is always there; all we have to do is look. Our kids can see at any moment the number of "friends" they have, "likes" they've received, replies to texts or chats that come in, and the time it takes for people to respond to them. Having more friends means that people like them. Having more "likes" means people like them. Receiving quick replies to texts means people like them. Too bad it never seems to be good enough.

If a kid has one hundred friends, they'll want 200 friends. If they receive "likes" on their posts, they'll want more. They'll question why someone takes ten minutes to reply, because usually they reply in five minutes. This focus on others behaviors coupled with an incessant flow of flawed data is making our kids miserable. My husband calls it an avalanche of crap that our kids have difficulty outrunning.

As a parent, I definitely struggle with how to handle my kids' use of online media. The truth is that it isn't all bad, just like it isn't all good. While it may not be the sole cause of escalating emotional issues amongst our children, it sure doesn't seem to be helping. When a child is suffering with emotional turmoil, throwing them into an environment where they can't see who's behind the screen to get a feel for intent from visual cues or tone of voice seems like a poor choice. Since we cannot insulate our children from online media entirely, I continue aiming to be the person my kids confide in when things get tough so they can learn how it feels to experience unconditional love, trust, and safety in their lives, and hopefully they can learn healthy online behavior through limited exposure, practice, and honest conversations.

Words From Piper
Why Can't I Be Like Her?
I want to be like her
I want my legs to look like two skinny poles
I want my stomach to be paper thin
I want my collar bones to stick out
I want people to whisper behind my back about how skinny I am
I want to be that girl
Well guess what?
You can be that girl now
You can have a tube shoved down your throat
You can have IV's stuck in your veins

You can be the one with a heartbeat of 50
You can be the girl in hospital bed
You can be her
But just remember there is always 2 sides to every person

Steps for Moving Forward:

1. Model the behavior you want your kids to develop. If you want them to learn how to create deep relationships and strong friendships, then you can show them how you do that with your own friendships.

2. Discuss how social media impacts your life and share openly how you feel about it. Ask them how they manage their own social media issues. In order to preserve the relationship with your child and teach them how to navigate the world of online media, focus on being a guide for them rather than the police.

Exercises:

1. Develop a family agreement around screens and social media. For example, my family agrees that there will be no screens after eight o'clock on the week nights.

2. Try a social media diet *with* your kids, i.e. one day, one week, or one month. Share your insights with each other.

Section III

Parenting Perspectives

Chapter 6

You Can't Pour from an Empty Cup

When I'm in the midst of a crisis with my daughter and someone mentions to me the importance of self-care, I kind of want to punch them in the throat. When my daughter is off her medication, has run away from school, or I am getting calls from her therapy team that she's feeling suicidal, I'm not running off to the spa for a mani/pedi.

During the times I'm just trying to keep my head above water, I think of self-care as allowing myself to do the basics. I try to eat three meals a day. Even if I can't make those meals terribly healthy, I still get something in my body. I try to go to bed at a reasonable time, even if I can't sleep right away. I try to say no to things, even if I want to say yes, because I know I am in crisis mode and need to unload my plate as much as possible. I try to spend time in stillness, even if it's only for a minute since it helps me reboot. Self-care can mean many things for different people, but when we are in crisis, it's all about the basics.

H.A.L.T.

I'm a member of Al-Anon, which is a support group for family and friends of alcoholics. They have an acronym for taking care of yourself: H.A.L.T. It stands for Hungry, Angry, Lonely, or Tired. It reminds us to watch ourselves when we are feeling any of these four things. It really served me when my husband was in the depths of his alcoholism, and I find it resurfacing now as I am weathering the storm of a teenager with intense, emotional struggles.

Hungry

My mom always said she thought I had a blood sugar issue. As a child, I would get really emotional and reactive when I was hungry. While I don't remember that, I do remember being intensely hungry and thirsty during my breastfeeding years. A shift would happen and suddenly I would become simultaneously ravenous and parched. I would mow over anyone or anything in my way to get my hands on food and water. The term "hangry" barely scratches the surface of the discomfort I was experiencing. I kid you not that there were times when I cried because of my hunger and thirst frustrations. I lashed out, was impatient, and, here's the fun part, felt terrible about myself after I was satiated.

Fast-forward to today. I no longer become "hangry," but I do notice that when I am hungry, I can be testy, moody, and easily irritated. Recently, I was taking a client phone call in my car. I had dropped off my daughter at school, and then found a lovely neighborhood nearby to park and settle in for my session. About forty minutes into the call, I noticed a young lady walking down the sidewalk who looked just like my daughter—because it *was* my daughter.

I immediately felt adrenaline coursing through my body. I became tense and scared and angry and frustrated and surprised and worried all at the same time.

As I continued to watch her walk away from me, I tried to stay present with my client on the phone. But then my daughter took a turn away from the school, and I realized she was not taking a break, but was running away from school. Alas, I slowly pulled up beside her, signaled for her to get her bottom into my passenger seat, and indicated for her to be quiet since I was on a call.

She got in and quietly sobbed while I wrapped up my session. She shared with me that she no longer cared about her life or where she was going. More adrenaline shot into my system and my mind was on fire with fear. Because I hadn't slept enough the night before or eaten a proper breakfast, I was pretty short with her. I had no interest in validating her feelings, understanding her situation, or compromising on a solution. Instead, I told her to "stop playing games." It was my fear, my worry, and my irritability talking—not my unconditional love for her.

She said nothing as I delivered her safely to school, talked with the school counselor, and promptly left as I had another appointment. She was visibly distraught, but I couldn't deal with her in that moment because *I hadn't done the very basics for myself* that morning. Because my entire morning was booked, this detour with my daughter had me rushing from one appointment to the next without any thought about my own emotional and physical wellbeing. As I drove to my noon appointment, my poor stomach was in disarray. Stress causes my tummy to do flip flops, and I hadn't eaten enough at breakfast to make it the entire morning. Add in the shots of cortisol and adrenaline and it felt like a small war had broken out inside of me. Thankfully, my client and I decided to meet in a coffee shop, where I could wolf down a sandwich and get my insides back on track before starting my appointment.

After my session and meal, I felt some relief. Some of the stress diminished and my stomach stopped doing cartwheels. And this is when the shame and guilt sets in. I felt awful about the way I treated my daughter, and the self-berating began. I wondered how I could have handled it better, if she needed something from me that I didn't give to her, or if I may have put a wedge in our relationship. As I got into my car to drive to my next appointment, I decided to send the following text to my daughter:

Me: I want you to know that no matter what you do or say, I will always love you. I believe in you! I know deep in my heart and gut that you are going to make it out of the muck of this time of your life, and you will use these experiences to make the world a better place. (heart emoticons)

I can't help but wonder what might have happened if I'd said this to her when I found her running away from school, or if I would have validated her feelings, or if I would have given her a hug and taken her home. Alas, we can't go back in time. All I can do is make amends and learn how to do better next time. Therefore,

I try to be very present to my own need and have some type of sustenance with me at all times, because I never know when there might be another crisis.

Angry

I remember being told that anger is a cover-up for fear when I was in therapy. This really resonated with me, because I will go from zero to ten on the anger scale when I am scared of something. When my mama bear persona kicks in because of a fear I have about one of my kids, watch out! I have behaved in ways that are incredibly unkind and ruthless when I am swimming in fear and anger. After being a part of Al-Anon, I came to realize that I wasn't the only one.

When things with my daughter escalate, I can very quickly catastrophize and awfulize all the terrible things that are going to happen in the future. This stirs up my fear and flips my anger switch to the "on" position. Because I don't want to feel the discomfort of what is happening, I will look for a place (read: person) to discharge my anger. If you happen to be in the room, then you might become my target. Just ask my kind and patient husband of twenty years.

One morning before school, my daughter decided that she wasn't going to go. I'd been struggling with stress for a couple of weeks. Not only was I intensely worried about my daughter, but my son was having some difficulties in school, work was really busy, and my school board responsibilities skyrocketed as we were hiring a new Superintendent. I hadn't cared for myself well through all of this stress and I was already feeling overwhelmed. When she informed me that she was staying home no matter what I said, my anger switch clicked.

When I am not taking care of myself, the time it takes for my brain to escalate to anger is miniscule. So, I yelled at her and said some things that were hurtful. I was discharging my fear, anger, worry, and frustration at her.

In the moment, I felt completely justified in my behavior. How dare she throw a monkey wrench into all the progress she has made? What does she expect me to do? How will she ever learn? How can I fix her? Why can't we just be normal? These are the thoughts that rush at me, and, at times, I have a hard time managing them and desperately look for a way to release them.

Then, as you might have guessed, comes the shame and embarrassment and guilt at how I've behaved. Follow that with some self-deprecating flagellation and you've got a perfect cocktail of self-loathing and misery. Even though I could apologize and try to make things right with my daughter, I cannot undo the damage my anger caused to our relationship. We may be able to overcome it, but neither one of us will ever forget it. It will forever serve as a chink on the armor of our connection.

I have gotten much better at shutting my mouth when I am angry. I now have a one-step process that goes like this: step one, breathe deeply in through my nose and slowly out through my mouth. I can repeat this single step until the anger dissolves. And it always does. Since I've started this practice of breathing through my anger, I find the dissipation happens really quickly now. If this step doesn't work for some reason, then I go to plan B: shut my mouth.

Allison's Golden Rule: Never say something you will have to apologize for later. Better yet, shut your mouth until something nice can come out of it.

Lonely

I remember back when my husband was still drinking there was nothing lonelier than being with someone with whom you can't connect. I was terribly lonesome, which resulted in me accepting behaviors I normally wouldn't. I befriended the wrong people because I desperately wanted to connect with someone, anyone. I tolerated my husband's bad behavior because I was terrified of being alone. I said yes to things because I couldn't stand the thought of being with myself, which is one of the root causes of loneliness. I couldn't be alone, because then I'd be forced to spend time with me—and I hated me.

Humans crave social connection, and this is even more prominent for adolescents. I have witnessed both my children tolerate bad behavior from their friends because they feared being lonely.

Once, our daughter had a friend, and we could see that she and my daughter were not good for each other. They tended to get into trouble when they were together, and there was always some kind of drama occurring between the two of them. I was particularly concerned because I witnessed my daughter's friend manipulate, lie, and cheat on multiple occasions. Even though I brought these incidents to my daughter's attention, she defended her friend and refused to consider distancing herself.

After about six months of their friendship, I received a call from my daughter's school to inform me that a teacher had been told by another student that our daughter was being abused. The school official shared that a full investigation had been made with the student who made the allegation, and they were confident that it was false. I was being told because the student who made the allegation would probably share it with our daughter since they were friends, and the official wanted me to know that they were on top of the situation.

Since I had an inkling the student who made the allegation was this particularly troublesome friend, I decided to do an investigation of my own. It turns out that I was right, which made me even more concerned for my daughter.

If you have a teen who is emotionally struggling, then you know how vulnerable they can be. My daughter was in the midst of tackling uncontrollable emotions, without any knowledge of how or when she would be able to feel normal again. She feared being alone more than she feared what this friend could do to her and her family. So, when I share what happened, I wasn't entirely surprised when, once again, my daughter defended her friend. While heartbreaking, I also understood. I, too, had tolerated bad behavior from loved ones in my life. Enabling is such an ugly behavior and it doesn't serve either party, yet, when we are lonely, we can make a great case for enabling bad behavior because the alternative is too difficult.

If someone can't stand to be alone, it may be they don't like themselves. The path to overcoming loneliness usually involves learning how to enjoy who we are, and how to be okay in solitude. For me, this meant looking in the mirror and committing to changing the things I didn't like about myself. For an adolescent, this is a difficult ask. My daughter has not yet learned how to identify and channel her superpowers, so she gets easily steamrolled by other teens, her own intense emotions, and her ego. When she does commit to changing things in her life for the better, she gets to experience the relief of feeling better about who she is and actually liking the person looking back at her in the mirror.

Tired

I have a workout partner who is the mother of four young children and I received a text the other morning that read: "Is it possible to die from sleep deprivation?"

There are few levels of exhaustion more intense than that of the sleep-deprived parent. I can remember pulling out of the garage half-asleep and ripping off my car's side mirror, pouring orange juice in my cereal, and aimlessly wandering the house forgetting what I was supposed to be doing. Adding any extra stress when I was already utterly drained had me in tears and throwing up my hands in surrender.

The first time I took my daughter to the hospital because she was suicidal, I experienced fatigue of a whole new realm. My husband happened to be out of town on a business trip, so I was home alone with both of my kids. As we were prepping for bed, my daughter ran into my room panicked about her thoughts of killing herself. I had her sleep in my room that night and slept with one eye open to make sure she was okay. She did try to leave the room several times in the night, but each time I was able to talk her into staying with me to be safe.

Needless to say, the following day, I felt like a zombie. Not only had I missed an entire night's sleep, but the emotional strain of what was happening with my daughter took a big toll. I had never been through this before, so I sent her to school the next day secretly hoping that it was just anxiety and she would be fine. We happened to have a therapy session scheduled that afternoon. No sooner had she gone into the office than the counselor came out to get me and have me join them in her room. She informed me that my daughter was to be taken straight to the ER about twenty miles north, since that hospital had a child psychiatric ward. She packed us both in my car and bid us farewell.

Stunned and still reeling from the night before, I hopped onto the highway with a flurry of thoughts racing around my mind. What do I do about my son who is home alone? What is a child psych ward? Will they keep her overnight? Days? Weeks? Are there straightjackets and padded rooms? Will I be able to see her?

By the time we got to the hospital, both my daughter and I were engulfed in fear. I was crying and couldn't hide what I was feeling. She, too, was terrified. Neither of us knew what to expect, and I was not in a place physically or emotionally where I could manage the situation. So, we sat in the parking lot at the hospital for a good thirty minutes crying and trying to muster the strength to go inside.

We did, eventually, go inside, got admitted, and then proceeded to wait for about six hours, as I explained in an earlier chapter. There were no beds available at that hospital. Who knew that there was a major shortage of mental health facilities for children? I had a long time to wallow in my own disappointment of how I had handled the situation. I had worsened my daughter's fear because I was so tired that I couldn't put on a brave face for her. I beat myself up for not being stronger for her and for myself. I raged against myself for not rising to the challenge. I can still feel the tension in my body when I think about sitting in that ER, dreading what was to come next.

Unfortunately, the story doesn't end there. At about midnight, we received our marching orders to have my daughter admitted to a hospital about two hours south. They handed me a packet of paperwork and told me to get going because the other facility was waiting for us. After driving in the middle of the night with ice on the roads and stray deer crossings, we arrived at the facility only to find that they no longer had a bed for her. We were sent to yet a third facility another hour away, where we arrived just before sunrise. As I was invited to say goodbye to my daughter, I found myself too tired to hold myself together. I fell to pieces as I hugged her and left her standing alone in a foreign place, filled with strangers, feeling totally scared and vulnerable.

As I left that hospital, I had literally been awake for over forty-eight hours. I was overcome by a tidal wave of emotions and I think I may have sobbed for the entire two-hour trip home. I still get squeamish when I think about that night. I know that I didn't have anything left to give. I always ask myself, if I'd had a full night's sleep, would it have mattered? Maybe not. I was pretty raw, and I can't imagine I wouldn't have imploded at some point during that evening. I do know, however, that when I do get enough sleep, I can slow my brain down and make better decisions. Instead of letting fear run the show, I can tap the brakes once in a while and see what other thoughts come forward.

Self-care comes in all shapes and sizes. When crisis lands on your shores, self-care is all about the basics. Eat food. Breathe. Love yourself. Sleep. Having the ability to slow things down is the key to making good decisions. The brain stem is easily triggered, which starts a domino effect in your body as it calls for hormones that prep the body for fight or flight. Having the ability to slowly nudge the amygdala back to sleep can greatly improve outcomes. And by caring for ourselves, we can eliminate the stages of self-berating after behaving in a fashion unbecoming to who we want to be.

Words from Piper
Save Myself
I stepped on the scale
But the number didn't drop enough

Failure
That was what I was
I didn't do good enough
The number was never good enough
The calories were always too much
My thoughts consumed every part of me
Head to toe
Don't eat that
That has too many calories
Throw that up
You're a pig
I was gone
I was far gone
And nothing could bring me back except for myself
I had to save myself

Steps for Moving Forward:

1. Bring some awareness to when you become hungry, angry, lonely, or tired. What do you notice about yourself? What kinds of decisions do you make? How do you feel about yourself? By becoming familiar with how you feel when you are hungry, angry, lonely, and tired, you can start to head things off at the pass.

2. Model the basics of self-care. When those around us notice how we seem to manage our lives well, even in the midst of crisis, they can be motivated to do the same for themselves. For instance, while my kids might poke fun at my senior citizen bedtime, they tend to mimic me by going to bed at a reasonable time without being prompted.

Exercises:

1. Next time you feel yourself escalating emotionally, remember to H.A.L.T. and determine if there is a basic need to be addressed, like eat, breathe, love, or sleep.
2. Reflect with the family on how H.A.L.T. worked for each of you during the day.

Chapter 7

Belonging and Acceptance

For as long as I can remember, I have yearned for belonging. The emotional pain I suffered yearning for that belonging can be strong even today if I am not present and conscious to what I am thinking. I spent about forty years of my life seeking the acceptance of my parents, only to come to two realizations. The first was that they were never going to accept me for who I am. The second was that it didn't matter. They may have been my family of origin, but I didn't belong with them. Therefore, I've surrounded myself with people who have similar values and mindsets as myself, unconditionally accept me, and provide me with a judgment-free space. Once I started to feel I belonged and was accepted, a deep need inside of me was satisfied.

Insurance Issues

During the process of writing this book, our daughter was prematurely discharged from a teen day treatment program that helped her learn and practice skills to deal with depression and anxiety. I received a call on a Tuesday around three o'clock from my daughter's day treatment therapist. She reported that our insurance company was no longer going to cover the day treatment costs. In fact, today was the last day of coverage. She assured me they could throw together a quick goodbye party for her before she had to leave at four o'clock. There was a long silence while I tried to process the information.

I asked how this could happen so quickly. Why weren't we informed at least twenty-four hours in advance? How was the insurance company making the determination that my daughter should be discharged immediately? How will we break the news to our daughter, who was not exactly in a good place? What will I tell her? How will I keep her from sinking into another depression? How is this the system?

The therapist offered little help. She said that the day treatment team saw no improvement in our daughter, so their reports to the insurance company were probably the reason coverage was being stopped. She confirmed that they didn't have a plan for transitioning her back to school. She was unable to answer my questions, and she became defensive (which was probably the result of my inquisition-style attack). She did mention that we could pay out of pocket to keep her in the program until Friday, which I agreed to do. This bought us time to get some other support systems for in place for our daughter.

As we concluded the phone call, the therapist said she'd tell Piper that she was being discharged. After the call, I had a session with a client, so I decided to send my daughter a text to let her know that I was not going to abandon her. It basically said that I loved her to pieces, and we would figure out how to move forward. By the time my husband arrived to pick her up, she was in a complete panic.

See, her therapist didn't tell her about the discharge as she promised, so our daughter found out through a surprise text from me. Because she couldn't get in touch with me, she escalated and was hyperventilating and sobbing as she got in the car that afternoon with her dad.

In the meantime, I was experiencing my own breakdown. I was confused and angry. I wondered why there were such big discrepancies between what we observed with our daughter versus what the day treatment staff saw. I was frankly pissed that they were so focused on the behaviors they weren't seeing from her rather than focusing on the things she was doing well. I scoffed at how this program was using the self-reporting of a thirteen-year-old child to monitor her progress. I was looking for someone or something to blame for the pain I was feeling, because, deep inside, I wondered what the heck was wrong with my daughter. She was feeling rejected and it literally hurt my heart to watch her experience this agony. I also felt like a failure as a mother, since I couldn't "fix" her either. Just like my daughter, I rushed into the misery of personalizing the discharge and making it mean that we were hopelessly broken.

Acceptance

Our daughter has lived through lots of rejection in her young life. Her peers don't understand her, so they often pull away when she is feeling out of control. We've also been told by other parents that they don't want their child hanging out with our daughter since she was hospitalized, as though her emotional turmoil is contagious. Her teachers are uncomfortable and treat her as though she is fragile and breakable. She's had only a few instances of true acceptance, and the rarity of it has hardened her edges.

When our daughter is excluded in any way, she feels like there is something inherently wrong with her. It seems to her that everyone else gets along and she's the only outcast. Of course, that isn't true, but her perceptions are her reality. As she grew older, if she had the slightest inkling that a friend was pulling away, she would switch into hyperdrive. She would quickly reject them before they could reject her by ending the relationship, saying terrible things, or asking for them to prove that they still cared about her. For her, this felt better than waiting to see if her friend was truly rejecting her.

So, when our daughter found out that she was being discharged quite suddenly from a day treatment program that she felt was supporting her, she fell apart. She asked what was wrong with her, why people were giving up on her, and what she could do to get back in their favor. She was desperate to fix herself, because she assumed that she was the problem. She became suicidal and shared that she didn't believe that she would ever find a place in this world where she would belong.

In her thirteen years on this planet, she's encountered repeated rejections, so it makes sense that she had so little faith. We talked a lot about how she was feeling during the three days leading up to her discharge from the treatment program. She was able to feel all the feelings that go along with being forced into a decision for reasons outside of her control. She had to face all the pain of wondering why things happened this way, how to say goodbye to everyone in the program, and how to move forward when she didn't feel ready.

By the time Friday came around, she was prepared for the difficult day ahead. It was tough, but she survived.

Rejection

As I am raising a daughter who struggles, I am so thankful for anyone who can offer us help and support. When the treatment program discharge happened so unexpectedly, I felt as though the rug was pulled out from under me. I had relaxed because I saw this program as a backup to the support systems we had in place at home and in school. Without warning, these people were rejecting both my daughter and me. I needed their help. I needed their support. I couldn't do this alone.

Interesting how we went to rejection first, right? My first thought was to wonder what was wrong with my daughter and me. I could have just as easily wondered what was wrong with the program or the insurance company. I could have even gone one step further and accepted that this program and our daughter were not a good fit, so it was just as well that we go our separate ways—but I didn't.

Most of my life, I felt like a square peg trying to fit into a round hole. I lived with a lot of rejection in my childhood, and it taught me to fit in at all costs. When I was rejected, I would figure out how to be what others wanted me to be, and then be that. I ignored who I was and what I needed. Being rejected showed me that I was wrong, so I did what I had to do to be right in the eyes of those around me.

By the time I was in my late thirties, I could finally recognize that I was living a lie. I was hiding who I was and lived in constant fear of being rejected by others. When I discovered that I could be myself without being rejected, it was like I could finally take off the masks I'd been wearing my whole life and relax. And when I discovered that the round holes were okay too, I really began to thrive. There was never anything wrong with me *nor* the round holes. We just didn't work together, and that was okay. In fact, it helped me learn how to love and honor people who didn't belong with me, which really helped me reconnect with members of my family.

Opportunity

As I spoke with some of my colleagues about what was happening with the sudden day treatment discharge, a few of them remarked that the universe seemed to be leading us elsewhere. As outsiders, they could see how this decision might provide us with an opportunity or a gift. If getting discharged is the thing that needed to happen so we could find something that better suited for our daughter, then the sooner it happened, the better.

When things happen to us, we often take it personally. We cannot see outside ourselves and a third party can provide us with perspective. This situation with my daughter reminded me, once again, that when something happens that I view as emotionally hurtful, I need to breathe, step back, and look at it outside of myself. By bringing in trusted outsiders, I can discover different ways to look at the situation and learn to see it from a more objective and open perspective.

In our eighteen months of obtaining mental health services, I have come to the conclusion that they are limited, mostly based on cognitive behavioral therapy models, and almost immediately utilize pharmaceuticals. Our daughter has been provided services at four different hospitals, as well as multiple day treatment and therapy programs. We've found that these services are essentially the same, the only difference being the location in which they are offered. A program over here being better than a program over there has not been true for us. With everyone seeming to offer the same approach, what do you do when that approach doesn't seem to be working?

Now, we are in search of different approaches. We are looking into functional medicine doctors, holistic wellness practitioners, and even spiritual guides. While our daughter is not ecstatic about trying these alternative approaches, she is open to meeting with these folks. If we should find some ways that provide her with relief amongst these approaches, I don't really care if they are considered "woo-woo." My daughter's discharge from the day treatment program may very well be a gift in disguise.

Are we "silver-lining" this dark cloud? Maybe. But, here's the thing. Spending time and energy being upset over something we can't control only makes us feel worse. It doesn't change the fact that she no longer has a program to attend. She *has* to transition whether she likes it or not. When we focus on what we can do next, it helps us get out of a victim mentality into one of empowerment. Sure, we still have some negative emotions associated with everything that happened, but we don't have to linger longer than necessary. If she is a square peg, then let's stop trying to shove her into round holes. We need to find some square ones instead.

Judgment

I make a living working with people who think differently. These people are always challenging the status quo and they never run out of ideas. The irony isn't lost on me that I have a daughter whose brain also works differently than most and I struggle to help her see her uniqueness as a superpower. The one commonality between my clients and my daughter—and even myself—is that we fear judgment. That fear of being judged has us hiding who we are, keeping our amazing ideas to ourselves, and wondering what is so wrong with us that we can't be like everyone else.

When our daughter began cutting herself, we were very careful not to react dramatically. Like I addressed earlier, I know how crippling shame can be, so I would calmly bandage her wounds and tell her that cutting is just a coping tool. Because she didn't feel judged by me, she could come to me when she was scared and overcome with intense emotions. She never had to hide her actions from me. She is still alive because when her coping tools escalated to suicidal thoughts and actions, she felt that she could tell me that she'd swallowed a bottle of pills.

Withholding judgment when my child's life is on the line is incredibly difficult. The voices in my head scream at me.

Who does she think she is?
What the heck did she do this time?
Doesn't she realize that this is tearing our family apart?
How many more times is this going to happen?

Like the duck who seems calm on the surface, but whose feet are paddling like mad under the water, I can love my daughter through her pain even though my insides are going bananas. But in order to do this, I have to commit to not judging her. This commitment means I cannot go around the emotions and my discomfort by blaming, shaming, and judging, but, instead, I must go *through* them. That means I have to feel my feelings and be conscious and present, so I can see my daughter as the beautiful young woman she is.

For me to withhold judgment of my daughter, I'm learning that it starts with withholding judgment of myself. When she is hurting herself, it hurts me too. I don't like pain, so I look for a place to discharge the discomfort. The ego part of my brain is only too happy to help and starts ramping up all the thoughts that excuse me from feeling uncomfortable. *It's social media, American culture, public education, smartphones, middle school girls, the breakdown of the nuclear family, Hollywood, or unskilled therapists at a day treatment program who are more concerned with getting insurance to pay for their services than they are about the children they are charged with supporting.* If my discomfort were a hot potato, I would toss it to any one of those thoughts and feel completely and self-righteously entitled to do so. But for me to take back my power, I have to hold the hot potato and work through the pain. I can then let the hot potato go, not into someone else's hands, but into a pot or oven, where it can be transformed into something useful.

For example, I notice how often I describe my daughter as having a mental illness. "Oh, she's probably depressed or bipolar," I explain. It's gratifying when people nod their heads in understanding, as though identifying her as one of "those" people puts her in the box of the mentally ill. I do this to lessen my own judgment of my parenting because I feel so much shame, embarrassment, failure, weakness, and self-loathing when I think about the ways I've let my daughter down. Putting a label on her is a great way to take all those feelings, shove them in a bag, and toss it out the window: "Oh, she's bipolar. So, you aren't a terrible mother and failure as a parent; she was born with this affliction. Nothing you could do, Allison."

The truth is that my daughter is a beautiful young woman who sees, feels, and thinks differently, which is not a bad thing. It's just different. Just like when I was young and I thought differently, I put a lot of pressure on myself to hide my thoughts and feelings for fear of being rejected. Unfortunately, our culture often marginalizes people who think differently, which I experienced personally. As my daughter now travels that same path of being different, she is learning this lesson as well.

Every new doctor or therapist visit—which, let me assure you, is plenty—starts with the question of her diagnosis. I have found that my daughter's diagnosis has more to do with the doctor we are seeing than it does with her symptoms, i.e. five different hospital psychiatrists equals five different diagnoses. And then there are the therapists and school counselors and well-meaning family members and friends with some acquaintance who had similar symptoms who was diagnosed with something totally different than what everyone thought and so on. But isn't the diagnosis—a label—in itself a judgment?

What does the label do for us and for her? Does it excuse certain behaviors, elicit immediate sympathy, or drive people away? For my daughter, the label is a scarlet letter. At times, it absolves her of all responsibility and has her raising her hands in surrender. Other times, she uses it as a way to find answers to what is going on in her mind. And yet other times, she uses it as a sword to hurt and maim.

Just this morning, the CBS Sunday Morning show reported on the different aspects of mental illness. It hit me that our culture considers it an illness when someone has a way of being that is outside the range of what most of us experience. For instance, they showcased a man who had a head injury that caused him to struggle with everyday cognitive abilities, but he could mold a beautiful, 3D model of an animal out of clay in fifteen minutes. Is he mentally ill or does his brain access parts that most of us cannot? If my daughter is able to access the deeply intense emotional centers of her brain, then calling it an illness minimizes her worthiness. If her brain operates at different wavelengths than her peers, perhaps we can honor that and get curious about it instead of labeling it. If we can withhold judgment about how she experiences the world, then maybe she would find more opportunities for belonging and acceptance. When we stop judging others, we stop judging ourselves and we, too, can find belonging and acceptance.

Words from Piper

Dear Ex-Best Friend
It's been a few months
How are you?
Do you still break people?
Am I offending you?
Well here's the truth
I was the glue to our friendship
I was your tv, your entertainment
You threw me in the trash like a piece of paper
I was a clown to you, you would always laugh at me
I was your toy, the toy you broke in half
That's the truth
Goodbye

Why?

Why did you choose me?
How could you?
You rejected me
After everything we've been through

Yet you still leave every time
You treat me like a princess one moment
And like a disappointment the next
You don't give a crap
And you never did
I'm sorry I wasn't enough
Wait
Why am I apologizing?
You were the one who broke me into a million pieces
So there you have it
The truth
You rejected me
Bye

Steps for Moving Forward:

1. The biggest impact we have on our children's lives is how we make them feel. Consider your impact on how your children feel. Do they have to perform to receive your attention? Do they have "deserve" a reward or acknowledgment? Do they feel worthy just for being themselves?

2. When situations get difficult and you take things personally, model for your children how you can breathe, step back, and seek an objective perspective.

Exercises:

1. Reflect on where you fit in versus where you belong. Pay attention to your behaviors in each of these environments. Fitting in usually means you have to change who you are, whereas belonging is when you don't.

2. When you judge yourself harshly, try to flip the thought into a positive one. For example, "I am such an idiot!" can be flipped to "I just learned another way not to do something."

Chapter 8

The Parenting Must Go On

I f you have a child who fights to regulate their intense emotions, then you may feel like you are walking on eggshells all the time. The risks of upsetting an emotionally volatile teen are high. However, they still need guidance and boundaries and they need to be held accountable even if it distresses them. This is by far *the* most difficult thing for me. As a mother, part of my job is to both keep my daughter healthy and help her succeed on her own in the real world. Many times, I feel as though those two jobs are at distinct odds with each other. Parenting an adolescent with violent mood swings, self-harming tendencies, or suicidal ideations can be incredibly challenging.

School Sucks

Our daughter attends the public middle school in our town. Because she struggles with her emotions, rides the emotional roller coaster many times per week, and has distorted thoughts, many of her experiences at school have been negative and painful. After all, public education is not known for addressing the emotional and behavioral needs of our children well. In fact, there were times when she seemed completely traumatized by events she went through at school.

My daughter doesn't like to go to school, has trouble staying focused, and has to force herself out of bed on school days. When she refuses to go to school, I cannot force her. I've tried bribing, enabling, threatening, begging, and pleading. She will not budge.

When my daughter forgot to take her medicine for three days in a row, she began to unravel. Her thoughts became darker and her nervous energy was surging. She couldn't sleep at night and found it nearly impossible to go to school. One day, she looked me right in the eyes and stated that she was not going to school. I tried my usual strategies. When none of them worked, I came the realization that she was not going and there was nothing I could do about it. So, I said, "Because you are not incapable of going to school today, if you choose not to go, then I will not call school and have your absence excused. Unexcused absences usually result in a detention. Are you prepared for the consequences of refusing to go?"

She responded that she was prepared and that she didn't care.

I proceeded to get in my car with my son, and we left. I made sure all the sharp objects and medications were locked up and I said a prayer. My insides were all messed up, and I could feel the adrenaline and cortisol pumping through my body. I was scared that she would hurt herself. I was afraid she would never go to school again.

I was worried that I had abandoned her in her time of need. I had to make a decision in the moment and trust that it was the right one, but it sure had me turned inside out.

Because I had to work after I dropped off my son at school, I could not go home to check on my daughter. In midst of a work call that morning, I received a text from the school counselor.

Counselor: Piper's on the phone. She called school.

Me: Am with a client.

Counselor: Can I go pick her up?

My nervous system suddenly kicked into high gear. I completed my session and quickly called the school. It turns out that my daughter had called school because she was scared that she'd made a really bad decision. She stated that she was skipping school and realized she didn't want to skip after all. However, she didn't know what to do because she didn't have a way to get to school. The counselor and dean made the decision to go pick her up.

Emotions rolled over me like a tidal wave.

Pride
Shame
Humiliation
Relief
Gratitude
Embarrassment
Disappointment
Guilt

Also, my insides were a complete jumble from the stress of the morning, and I felt a little sick to my stomach. I thanked them profusely and then cried in my car.

The truth is that my daughter could have continued making bad decisions that day, but she didn't. I'd like to think that my intuition is good, that I somehow knew she wouldn't do anything risky or dangerous. But the fact is, I was never really sure. There are times when I feel certain that she will be safe, and there are times when I can tell she needs to be watched. Then there are times when I'm just not sure.

By being a parent in that moment, I was showing her that I wouldn't enable her to miss school. If her mind is in chaos mode, I can empathize with her inability to make good decisions. However, I try to let the natural consequences teach her. Sometimes a natural consequence will snap her out of her downward spiral and sometimes it doesn't. The natural consequences of not going to school are detention, missed work, and having to catch up the following day. She was fully aware of those penalties when she told me she wasn't going to school. It took her brain some time to process what was going on, but she was eventually able to turn her bad decision into a good one. She had dug herself into a hole, and I didn't intervene. It's a fine line how far we let our kids dig before we take away their shovel.

The bigger problem, of course, is how to help our kids who struggle emotionally to enjoy school. When they don't feel understood or their brains are distorting reality, they can feel like school is far too overwhelming. My daughter feels utterly disconnected with the people in her school. She doesn't trust her peers, because she doesn't believe they will like or accept her if they find out she self-harms or takes anti-psychotic medication or was hospitalized.

In the middle school environment, she changes classes every fifty minutes, so she doesn't get the opportunity to connect with her teachers. Likewise, middle school teachers are responsible for hundreds of students, so they are hard-pressed to connect with any one child. Her belief is that she is an outcast, and then she looks for proof each day that her belief is true. I just wish it weren't so easy for her to find that proof.

My daughter has tried online schooling, switching schools, 504 plans, and joining extracurricular activities. Thus far, we've not found anything that works well. So, I made the decision to tell her that she had to find a way to finish out the school year at her current school. My thought was that perhaps if she knew there was no way around her current situation, she would find a way to get through her school days. At times, I think she needs me to tell her the answer and then not budge. It's almost like I can feel her relief when she knows that I am not going to let her off the hook. This is the part of parenting that I hate. To make a decision, then watch as your child struggles over and over again. Because her pain causes me pain, I question the decision and want to make the pain stop. Yet, my daughter does better when I can commit to my decision and stand firm as her parent.

Friends and Frenemies

For a child who struggles to regulate her emotions, forming relationships with her peers has been difficult. We've found that the kids who are the most troubled tend to attract one another and stick together. While my daughter feels like she can be herself with other troubled teens, she also picks up some of their mindsets and values. As I've previously mentioned, I believe we are the average of the five people with whom we spend the most time, so it's critical for our daughter to cultivate relationships with emotionally healthy children. She cannot do this if she chooses kids who are depressed, anxious, and self-harming too.

When our daughter befriended a young lady who encouraged our daughter to break rules, be mean to other kids, and lie and manipulate to get what she wanted, we were less than pleased. We asked her about this friendship, and my daughter responded that she felt like she didn't have to hide all her scary thoughts from this friend. While I understood the need to be able to share with someone who can understand, I'm also old enough to know that my daughter could easily be manipulated by someone who only feigned understanding so she could have a partner in crime.

This relationship lasted for almost an entire school year. My daughter lost all of her other friends. She was self-harming more frequently. She spent more time on social media. She withdrew herself from the family. There were plenty of red flags. We knew that if we forbade her from seeing this friend, she would try to find ways to defend her. We wanted her to come to the conclusion on her own so she could learn this lesson herself. This girl played lots of games with my daughter, and each time my daughter would get hurt, she vowed to end the relationship. Yet, she had alienated all of her other friends, so she didn't have any support systems in place when this girl would come back, apologize, and start the game all over again.

It was very difficult to parent during that friendship. There were so many times when I wanted to just shut down the friendship and tell my daughter she could no longer be friends with this girl. But the reality is that they were at school together, so she could hang out with her friend there. They also had cell phones, so they could continue to communicate with each other that way as well.

So, each time our daughter got hurt by this friend, we would pick her up, put her back together, and make the point that the friendship didn't seem to be a good one for her. Eventually, she did break up with this friend. And the important part is she chose to do it on her own, without any help from us. It was really hard for her, but she is stronger and smarter as a result of doing it herself rather than having us do it for her.

Boundaries

In Al-Anon, learning to set boundaries for behavior that is and is not acceptable changed everything for me. We learned that it was counterproductive to clean up an alcoholic's mess, regardless of how big and destructive it might be. It was because of being in Al-Anon that I learned to set boundaries and defend them, which has come in very handy for dealing with my daughter.

There was a post last week in a parenting support group about how to deal with foul language if a child is suffering from a mental illness. This parent wondered if they should punish their child, who was lashing out from high intensity emotions. The responses were all over the map. Some parents said to punish the child. Others said that the child cannot control themselves, so punishment was unjust.

Personally, I believe that if a child cannot regulate their thoughts and emotions, foul language is a symptom. I can have compassion for my child and understand that she may be experiencing some emotional turmoil, but I don't have to tolerate being verbally assaulted. In those moments, when she crosses my boundary, I inform her that she stepped over a line and tell her to get back on the other side. If she refuses, then I excuse myself and go somewhere else. This diffuses the negative energy and also keeps both of us from saying things that may hurt the other.

My goal for my daughter is that she learn through experiences, not through punishments doled out by me. If she is looking for a place to discharge her negative energy, I can let her know that I understand why she's doing it and then remove myself from her line of fire. She learns that I won't be a target for her, which can be much more effective than grounding her or taking away her cell phone.

This approach works for social media, curfew, chores, etc. The boundary is the line that divides what is and what is not okay with me. When my child invades my boundary, I can usually let her know that she's doing so and then see if she can reel it back in. If she can, then she learns that she can regulate herself. If she can't, then she learns that I won't tolerate bad behavior. Some of my boundaries are stiff, while some are soft and squishy, but I must have them to be a good parent. In many ways, my daughter appreciates the constancy, stability, and security of knowing my boundaries and how I will defend them, regardless of what she does or says.

But, Mom, I Want It

Because my daughter gets tired of being depressed and unmotivated most days, she really gravitates towards immediate gratification. Because I get tired of watching my daughter suffering so much, I also find myself saying yes to things, even though I know the happiness she'll experience as a result is fleeting. When my daughter asks to go to Target and look around, I am usually game. And then I always wonder if I'm enabling her.

My daughter has shared that she self-harms because she feels like she deserves to be punished. It's never for anything in particular, but instead for general things, such as feeling like she's fat or doesn't have any friends. Worthiness is a tricky thing for teens.

For a parent, it can get a little confusing. I don't want to give my daughter everything she wants, because I want her to learn how to deal with disappointment, how to work hard for something, and the value of a dollar. At the same time, I don't want my daughter to ever feel like she has to earn worthiness because, of course, she is already worthy.

It's been a while since my daughter has had a string of successes. Momentum and inertia are real when it comes to motivation. It's like people have a threshold for failure before we just throw in the towel. So, I've been toying with intermingling small successes with small celebrations. The hope is that as these small successes start to pile up, she will gain momentum and not have to work so hard to get through her days.

Additionally, by celebrating her successes, we are acknowledging how she created the success by being her most wonderful self. In other words, she's worthy because she's alive. Then I can tie in a small reward to connect the idea of hard work with its resulting pay-off. The system isn't perfect, but it does help her focus on the small wins each day.

To address my fears around enabling her, I've decided to tell my daughter how I'm feeling. We talk about my worry of creating an entitled child who may never learn to work hard. She's always quick to point out how hard she has worked in the past and how hard she is working now, which is a great exercise for both of us. For her, she gets to acknowledge her own achievements. For me, I am reassured that she understands the risks of using rewards as an incentive for making good decisions. Plus, it's a blast when I get to be the student and my daughter can be the teacher. When I am open to the possibility that my daughter has loads of wisdom to impart, I find a gold mine of information, and our relationship deepens as a result.

High Risk

Let's just address the elephant in the living room, shall we? Because my daughter is suicidal and has attempted to kill herself multiple times, I view the risks of parenting very differently. If I give my daughter a consequence, or say no to a request, or refuse to tolerate bad behavior, then there is the risk that she might kill herself.

Of course, this risk is true for all parents, but it's acute for me since we've lived through the attempts. It's not crying wolf after five hospitalizations. What's a parent supposed to do when the risk of parenting has the potential to drive the child to act impulsively and recklessly?

Unfortunately, for me, the answer was to accept the fact that my daughter might succeed in dying by suicide. By giving up control of her will to live, I was able to walk through the pain and agony of the possibility of losing her forever. On my knees, with arms raised towards the sky, I begged my higher power to be with me in this darkest of places. Accepting a child's death before they have died is a tortuous affair. It hurts. A lot. But once I went through the dark place of sadness, desperation, grief, anger, and fear, I was able to weather the storms of parenting my daughter— and accepting the risk.

The same week that my daughter forgot to take her medications, and consequently unraveled, she had another incident at school when she left the building without telling anyone. I happened to be in the neighborhood and saw her walking down the street, so I was able to pick her up and return her to school.

It was in that moment that she came the closest to following through on her threat to drown herself. She was walking towards the bridge in our town that crosses a large river. After that day, I found myself panicking every time I crossed that bridge. I would shake, cry, and play a scene in my mind of her jumping off the bridge into the frigid water below.

Again, I had to go through the experience of accepting that she might die by suicide someday, and that I have no control over that. I have to go through the pain and acceptance again and again. I have to go through it every time we have another scare. But the reason I continue to make myself go through this process is so that I can love and care for her and parent her to the best of my ability. Parenting is loving my child unconditionally, allowing her to learn life's lessons, keeping her safe, and not enabling her to make bad choices. Thankfully, this practice has also resulted in me finding more moments of joy and laughter with my daughter. By allowing the intense negative emotions in, I allow the intense positive ones in too.

So, here's the summary on how I parent. I don't know what I am doing most of the time, but I try to trust and listen to my higher power. I try to lead with my heart when I'm in a quandary. I try to love her through the pain rather than recoil from the fear. I talk about what's happening with our daughter to lots of people to end the stigma around mental illness and find support and resources for all of us. At times, I'm too stern. Other times, I'm too lenient. I listen to wise people and shut out the rest. The most helpful thing I have found thus far is that getting in touch with my intuition is far more valuable than intellectualizing my daughter's situation. If I feel she's ready for a nudge, I give it. If it's a hug, then I'll do that. It it's a break, I can hit the pause button. If it's unadulterated acceptance, then I am the first in line. My goal is for my daughter to know that she is loved unconditionally and that I believe in her, even when she doesn't believe in herself.

Words from Piper
Letter to Mom
Dear mom
Thank you
For everything
You are my rock
You are my sunshine
You are the one that never gave up on me
You are always there
You are my best friend
You always know what to say
You are my protection
You help me through my bad days
You make the good days better
You give me light
You made me the person I am today
I love you mom

Steps for Moving Forward:

1. Notice when fear is driving parenting decisions. When fear and worry get in the way, it's helpful to take a deep breath, listen to your higher power, and lead with your heart.

2. Be open and honest with your child about your parenting choices. Model for them how you weigh all the factors and come to a conclusion, as well as how you can be open to changing a decision when you recognize it might need tweaking.

Exercises:

1. Get in touch with your heart or compassion. Spend a few minutes closing your eyes and breathing into the space of your heart each day. By practicing being in the heart space, it'll be easier to call it forward in moments of difficult parenting decisions.

2. Practice using your intuition by reflecting what you think your child is thinking or feeling, and then check for accuracy. For example, "Bobby, you seem a little unsettled. Am I reading that right?"

Chapter 9

Live Life Day to Day

Addicts and alcoholics got it right with their approach to life during recovery: take it one day at a time. When you find yourself being sucked into a crisis and your brain stem signals your body to get the cortisol and adrenaline pumping, it's very easy to lose yourself in fear, worry, and concern.

For example, when my daughter is imploding and does something really dangerous, I can remind myself to just get through the next minute, or the next hour, or until dinner. If one day is too big, then I break it into something I can manage. Sometimes I just need to get through the call with Poison Control, or the drive to the hospital, or making my bed in the hallway to prevent my daughter from running away. Breaking down my time or the tasks ahead of me interrupts my brain's natural inclination to run amok thinking of all the terrible things that could happen.

"What If" Thinking

"What if" thinking can be paralyzing when your child is struggling. You may use this type of thinking to put off vacations, make decisions about future investments, or prevent yourself from taking on professional obligations. It seems counterintuitive, but it has been my experience that being present in the moment helps me ward off the "what ifs." Fear drives me to want to know the future, but since I cannot know it, I can choose to let it go.

Of course, it's never as easy as just letting it go, like dropping a lovely feather on the ground. Instead, it is like clinging to the side of a rock wall, trusting that letting go won't end in total catastrophe.

Some of my fears for my daughter include more hospitalizations, residential treatment, suicide attempts, running away, self-harm, eating disorders, long-term damage from overdosing on pills, future drug and alcohol abuse, and forming dysfunctional relationships with peers. I can work myself into quite a lather if I entertain my fears. By choosing to be present in the current moment, I am able to ward off the big, hairy worries and concentrate on the here and now instead. I can find peace here, which is everything to a parent who never knows when the other shoe will drop.

As our daughter comes up on her last year of middle school, my "what if" thinking is all revved up for high school. She's essentially missed about two years of middle school, so my fear has me convinced that she'll flunk out of high school and end up homeless and living under a bridge, leaping ten steps ahead into a dark future. I can usually talk myself out of the last part, but the worry about her high school experience is very real. At this time, I cannot imagine how she will navigate high school pressures without ever being able to successfully navigate the pressures of middle school. The risks of failure increase, the pressure from peers is more pronounced, and high school begins the permanent record that determines secondary education and career paths.

Since I already know how to play the "what-if game" so well, sometimes I can use this same thought process to turn a negative into a positive. Instead of wondering "what if" she flunks a class or has friend issues, I can think about "what if" she figures out how to succeed in one class, or makes a nice friend, or joins a club, or goes out for a sport, or creates something really special. I can put my focus on all the ways she can win and then prepare myself to acknowledge her successes and celebrate them. Instead of going for only the home run and nothing less, she can be recognized for lots of base hits along her journey.

Distractions

There is no doubt that stress sends me spiraling into my own unhealthy coping habits. I come from a long line of problem drinkers, and I became one in my teens and carried it on until age 35. Therefore, I had to take booze off my list of coping tools. Smoking is off my list too (I have asthma and it's gross). This leaves other numbing activities, like food, social media, being too busy, and shopping. I typically choose food. It's delicious, readily available, and immediately gratifying. When the stress builds, I have no qualms about grabbing a spoon and a jar of Nutella and ingesting my painful emotions.

When I was a kid, I spent a lot of time alone. My folks divorced when I was young, so I came home to an empty house every day. I was not allowed to do sports because my mom couldn't pick me up after practice. I also wasn't allowed to have friends over unless my mom was home, which she never was because she had to support two children on her own. Alas, it was me, the Brady Bunch, and a pantry full of snacks. Food was comforting and it was my companion. I've used it as a copying tool my whole life. So, when chaos and crisis hit, it's easy for me to fall back into my relationship with my good pal, Food.

I've learned that food is really a distraction from the emotional discomfort I would rather avoid, along with working too many hours, binge-watching Netflix, and even doing one more load of laundry. By taking on all sorts of responsibilities, I create a life where I am too busy to sit with my emotional crap. There is always a way to put off a difficult conversation or ignore red flags with my kids. Distractions are wonderful because they allow me to skirt around the issues I don't want to deal with, and, bonus, they can be justified as "important" things that must get done.

Just like my daughter uses cutting, restricting her calories, and swallowing too many pills, I, too, have tools that offer me a way out of the pain that is right in front of me. It's why I can understand my daughter's struggle, as well as want desperately to make it disappear. None of us want to feel our negative feelings, especially when they are intense and uncomfortable. Just like nobody wants a root canal, but, at some point, action must be taken with the tooth. We can keep denying that the tooth hurts, but eventually the pain grows and can no longer be ignored. Emotions, when pushed down and ignored, eventually surface. They may not come out the way we expect, but they will present themselves. If we continue to distract ourselves, these emotions impact our nervous system, our health, our well-being, our relationships, and our ability to judge reality. Sitting in the pain and feeling the feelings is the only way through, just like the root canal. Even if we wish it weren't so.

Awfulizing

When my daughter is going through a rough patch, I can take the situation and run off at full speed into the future. When my daughter took a large number of pills with the intention of ending her life, I freaked out because my immediate concern was for her physical health and safety. But it didn't stop there. I awfulized the incident and worried that she would end up in an institution, never be able to have children, or have to eventually undergo a kidney transplant. I wondered if she would ever be able to face the challenges of life without becoming so overrun by emotions that she would end up living in our basement forever, dependent on us because she couldn't face the real world. I worried that her attraction to pills was a precursor to drug and/or alcohol addiction.

This awfulizing behavior is another behavior carried over from my childhood. My mother is a terrific awfulizer. I learned from a master, and I'm pretty darn good at it too. My mom used awfulizing to keep from being disappointed or taking responsibility and justify not changing. She passed the behavior down to me in many different forms. I was assured that when I had a conflict with a friend, I should let that friend go, because that person will just continue to disappoint me anyway. When my father disappointed me, my mom was quick to teach me that men could not be counted on, least of all my own father. When I discovered that my husband had developed a severe drinking problem, my mom was right there to advise me to leave him because he will only let me down again. While she may not have said these things out loud, it is her voice in my head that speaks to me when I am in crisis.

When my daughter first showed me that she was cutting herself, my mom's voice was very loud in my head. It was telling me that my daughter was just looking for attention; she was disappointing me, and she needed to grow up.

That voice is the starting line for the race to the future of doom and gloom. When I empower this voice and buy into what it's saying, I disconnect from my authentic self and my daughter. At a time when my daughter needs me to have compassion and love her unconditionally, I have to be kind to myself and leave the judgment, shame, and blame behind.

I don't begrudge my mother for her fear of risk or for using awfulizing as a coping tool to not get hurt. When her voice pops into my mind, I can understand that it is only trying to protect me, just like my mother was doing when she explained her version of the world. Her warnings and declarations of "how things are" were a way for her to pass along her wisdom. When we find something that works, we like to share it with others, especially those we love. However, when that voice no longer serves me, I want to have the courage to try a different path.

When my daughter struggles and does something dangerous, I have to acknowledge my mother's voice in my head, thank it for its input, and then choose a different voice to hear. With time and practice, I have been able to identify lots of other voices that are kind, wise, and gentle. These are the ones I reach for when my world is turning upside down. By connecting with these voices on a regular basis, I can find them much more quickly in times of high stress—the ones telling me to go slow, not to panic, to stay in the present, and, most importantly, to love my daughter unconditionally.

Be Present

The mindfulness movement has gained a lot of momentum because people feel significantly better after sitting in stillness and peace, even if it's only for a few moments. I love the feeling of relief when I can focus on the present.

When I started learning about mindfulness and different calming techniques, I had to practice the easiest ones first to get the hang of it. When crap hits the fan, it's too hard to try and remember more than one thing, so having a single go-to technique was critical for me. Mine was to take a deep breath in through my nose and out through my mouth, then another and another until I could calm down.

When I take a deep breath nowadays, I close my eyes and enjoy the feeling of filling my lungs, becoming aware of any tightness or stress in my body, and enjoying knowing how to just breathe through the chaos. My body and mind go into autopilot when I take a deep breath, and I am suddenly transported from a pain of the past or a catastrophe yet to happen to the present moment. It is such a gift to be able to pull myself from whatever time warp I'm engulfed in and deal with what is happening in the moment.

Bitter Pill

Mindfulness and being present in the current moment have changed for me since my daughter's first suicide attempt. When my child tried to end her life because she couldn't imagine living it anymore, I really struggled to keep myself out of both the past and the future. I felt the urge to constantly be on alert for any warning signs or red flags, lest I miss them, and she do something drastic. I thought about all the things she might try to do to herself, and created strategies for keeping her away from those things. I was always lurking, always noticing, and always watching her. She was irritated, and I was exhausted.

Not only was I not able to make her safer, I was eroding our relationship. She felt like I didn't trust her, and, therefore, she worried that she was someone who couldn't be trusted. When she felt like I didn't believe in her, she didn't believe in herself. When I treated her as though she were broken, she felt like there was something wrong with her. Yet, I reasoned the only way I could make sure she was safe was by hovering over her around the clock.

The truth that I came to accept and believe is that my daughter may hurt herself, may even end her life, and there is precious little I can do about that.

That statement is painful for me to accept, but I have accepted it. I can hide the sharp objects. I can lock up the medications. If she wants to do something badly enough, she will find a way to do it. For instance, we hid all the sharp objects in the house and locked up the medications, but my daughter was able to take a light bulb out of her lamp, break it, and use the shards to cut her arms. The bitter pill of reality I needed to swallow in order to move forward is that my daughter is only as safe as she wants to be.

Hiding things from my daughter only treats the symptoms, and I feel like it does make it safer for her. However, she is not safe just because we've locked things up. I find it's better to be closely attuned to her and use my intuition. While I cannot articulate how I sometimes know she is going to do something dangerous, while other times I feel very safe leaving her home alone, my intuition is usually right. By building a really close relationship with her, I can notice minor changes in her moods, language, and energy. This way, I'm not always on guard, but instead closely watching her only when she seems off. Not to mention, our deep bond is incredibly rewarding.

But let me clear that facing reality is really painful. I can avoid it, deny it, run away from it, sugarcoat it, or pretend that I don't see it, but I don't know any way around it. When I am ready to face reality, I know I will experience some gut-wrenching emotions. But once I get through that dark place and accept the reality in front of me, I emerge from the other side with a whole new game plan. My new strategy is to connect deeply with my daughter, remove all conditions for my love for her, and find as much joy and gratitude with her as I can muster each and every day. This is the bright side to taking on reality.

Reframe the Pain

When I find myself in a cycle of negativity, self-doubt, or worry, I try to find a way to reframe what is happening. Like the old saying goes, if you can't change your conditions, then change the way you think about them. I know that's easier said than done. But the beauty of being able to reframe my own perspective is that I can interrupt the thought pattern that keeps me circling the drain. When I can take a detour on my way to Awfulville, I experience relief and a feeling of being lighter. I can also be kinder to myself and am less likely to fall into shame and blame.

As my husband and I manage the stress of having an emotionally volatile daughter, our relationship has shifted substantially. We have moved from being able to support one another most of the time to distancing ourselves from each other often. We end up using a tag team approach to care for our daughter. For example, when she's feeling impulsive, I might sleep on the floor in her room to make sure she doesn't do anything to herself. The next day, my husband might take over more of the household duties recognizing that I didn't get a sufficient night's sleep. By the end of the next day, when I notice my husband's patience is whittled down to a tiny nub, I will pick up the slack, and so on. This is an appropriate strategy for momentary crises, but it isn't a healthy way to run a marriage. In many ways, this approach actually keeps us from connecting because one of us is always too exhausted.

I shared with a colleague my concerns about the tolls of raising a teen with emotional struggles on my marriage. I was worried that I would wake up one day and feel like my husband was a stranger. Our sex life had come to a screeching halt and I wasn't sure how to resurrect it, as I wasn't feeling particularly amorous most of the time. My colleague helped me reframe this by pointing out that my child is a product of my womb and it was natural to not be able to be aroused when your child is hurting. This one perspective changed everything for me. I didn't have to blame myself anymore for being too tired or selfish to be intimate with my hubby.

Another reframing that has unloaded the pressure for me is around what other people think of me as a parent. I am on the local school board, and I sometimes worry what people will say when they learn that my child has had multiple suicide attempts. I have become very involved with her schooling and making sure she receives the support she needs; yet, I still fear that some of these folks are just helping my daughter because I am on the school board. My way of reframing this is that we all have struggles in life, and I assume that these people care for me and my daughter. When I believe that people care about my family, I can let go of worrying what they say behind my back.

When all else fails in reframing my pain, I can always ask myself what this pain is affording me the opportunity to do. Usually I can find that I have something to learn and pain is part of the journey. When my child was released prematurely from her day treatment program, we decided that it was an opportunity to begin looking into alternative approaches. I can see opportunities really well when I can settle into my body and get out of my head. In fact, when I can really connect with my heart and my gut, I can usually see clearly what opportunities are right in front of me. Loving myself and my child is a great way to start getting a glimpse of all the options that are on the table, remembering to take things one day, one moment at a time.

Words From Piper

Why Me?

Why me?
Why do I have to go through this?
Lose friends?
Why am I the one like this?
I don't understand
And never will
A plan developed in my mind
If it doesn't get better should I be here?
I shouldn't

Steps for Moving Forward:

1. Notice if and how you might be distracting yourself from being present. The goal isn't to eliminate all distractions, but instead become aware of them.
2. Consider how you are facing your current reality. Accepting reality can be painful and uncomfortable, but it can lead to peace and serenity. It can be useful to do this work with a supportive network.

Exercises:

1. Try doing one thing at a time, like sitting down and eating a meal without any distractions, or taking a walk without

listening to a podcast, or standing in line and finding a way to enjoy the time.

2. Experiment with using your intuition with your child and others. Reflect what you are noticing about them and ask if you are correct.

Chapter 10

Allow Others to Love and Support You

think it's normal to feel shame and embarrassment when our child suffers from mental and emotional difficulties. We want to place blame and point fingers, which means that the fingers may end up pointing right back at us. I've been pleasantly surprised that when I let go of the need to blame, the shame and embarrassment subside. I have also found that when I share what is going on with my daughter with trusted friends and colleagues, I am enveloped in love and support. When someone offers to hug me, I let them. When I am crying and am offered a Kleenex, I accept it. When a person asks to pray for our family, I say yes. The result: I feel held and my heart is fuller.

What Can I Do?

When our lives are spiraling out of control and my daughter is going through some kind of crisis, I honestly don't know how to respond to the question everyone asks: "What can I do?"

My internal reaction is: What can this person possibly do for me? Are they neurologists that can understand what's happening to my daughter's brain? Can they make her feel better? Do they have the solution for why she is suffering?

But externally, I usually smile and respond with some kind of comment that we will all be okay.

I have two amazing friends who know everything. They are my running partners, and there's just no buffer when I'm gasping for air and every muscle, tendon, and ligament is screaming with pain. My running partners and I tell each other everything without any sugarcoating. They've put their hands on my back when I've had to stop running because I can't run and cry at the same time. I've shared my deepest fears with them. They know better than to ask what they can do, because they know there is nothing they can do, just like me. They feel helpless, just like me. They feel my pain, almost as intensely as I do. They never, ever try to fix or solve my problems, because they honor who I am and trust that I will eventually figure out my own solution. These women have carried me through some of the best and worst times of my life.

When the three of us decided to take a weekend trip to get away for a night, I was both elated and worried. While I desperately wanted to take a break from the stress and strain, I also knew that my daughter was not in a good place emotionally. Alas, I went anyways and gave my husband a condescending pep talk before I left (thankfully, he understood that the pep talk was for me more than for him). We were gone for about twenty-four hours, and it was just what I needed.

Even though my daughter had several issues while I was gone, my husband handled them. I was able to spend some time connecting with my dear friends, giggling until I wheezed, and blowing off some much-needed steam. These women knew that a night away was a reset button for me.

One of our conversations during that time away centered on trying to manage all the balls we had in the air. I mentioned that I was no longer able to make healthy meals for my family anymore and I was considering using a mail order food prep service. My friend looked at me and informed me that she wouldn't let me do such a thing. Instead, she would prep my meals for me since she loved my family and it was a small way that she could help me out. I thought it was a great idea since I already loved her cooking, so we worked out a deal and she's been prepping meals for us for months. Not only does she get to love us through her cooking, but we feel loved and supported by her every time we sit down to a meal that she's prepared for us. It's so much more fulfilling for both sides.

Now, when people ask me what they can do, I try to come up with something that I actually need. If my child needs a ride, I may ask if they know someone who can help me out. I may ask for a referral to a doctor or a nutritionist or an acupuncture practitioner. I might ask them if they know of another parent who's been through what I'm going through and if they could connect us. When I can't think of anything else, I ask them to say a prayer or send up some positive energy into the universe. It's just easier to have some things that you actually need ready to go when people ask, because most people honestly want to help, and it's up to you to give them the things you need.

I used to worry that people would feel put out or resentful if I asked them for help, but I realized that I was simply projecting my own issues onto them. In other words, I said yes to helping others because I wanted them to like me or I was trying to please them. Even if I didn't want to help or didn't actually have time to help, I still said yes, and then felt irritated at *them* because *I* had offered. When I stopped saying yes to things I didn't want to do, I was able to honor others' ability to do the same. If someone offered to drive my daughter, make me a meal, or just have a coffee with me, I stopped worrying if I was putting them out. My assumption is that these are all grown adults who will only say yes if they want to do something. If they don't, well then, that's their problem.

I Hate Pity

Nothing is worse than the look of pity when I'm in the midst of a bad spell. And there is a big difference between empathy and pity.

When I am feeling lost and scared, empathy is sitting in those feelings *with* me. Pity, on the other hand, is standing above me with a "that's too bad" or "sucks to be you" attitude, not really connecting with me.

Empathy is compassionate. I don't need those who are empathetic to say or do anything. It's just reassuring to know that I am not alone in this world. When I share my demons with others, I am looking for their love and kindness. If the comments I receive seem disengaged, I usually stop sharing and move on. I may even assure the pitying people that I will be fine, my daughter will be fine, that we will all be fine. It feels yucky to be on the receiving end of pity and sympathy, so I try to end the interaction as quickly as possible.

I have always scored high in empathy, which has resulted in being a compulsive people-pleaser for most of my life. Empathy is the ability to put myself in someone else's shoes, to feel their pain as they feel it. This is both a gift and a curse. The gift is that I can *be* with a person in their pain, and I have trained myself not to try to fix or solve their problems for them as a boundary for myself. The curse of empathy is that I pick up others' pain and carry it if I'm not careful. When my daughter hurts, I literally hurt too. I pick up on her subtle cues and start to internalize the impending doom. The only way for me to discharge the pain is to talk about it, and all I need is for the other person to listen with empathy. I guess I also like hugs. And chocolate.

My mother and father are really good at pitying. When I share what is happening with my daughter, they back away emotionally and disconnect. My mother responds with anger and insinuates that my daughter is simply looking for attention and manipulating me. My father does the "poor kid" routine and then asks how often she exercises. Neither approach is helpful, so I typically don't choose to discuss my daughter's condition with them.

I have shared with my mother that her pity is hurtful, and I would prefer empathy and compassion, but she doesn't know how to do that, so I don't have any expectations of her changing. If I worked really hard, I might be able to help her understand how to help me, but I'm already working hard at everything else and not inclined to take on another project. It makes me sad that my parents cannot help me, but I also accept that they aren't equipped to do so. I love them dearly, and I know they do the best they can.

Along those lines, I have found it helpful to respond to pity and sympathy with honesty. When someone says, "I don't know how you do it," I respond with the fact that I don't see another choice. Sometimes I will ask them what they'd do if they were me, which is my own empathy test of sorts. Other times, I just sigh and agree that life's tough. But by recognizing the folks who have empathy and compassion, I can intentionally seek them out, while also accepting that not everyone can "do" empathy and letting those folks off the hook for responding in a way that is not helpful.

It's Okay to Cry

I'm an ugly crier. My face crinkles up, my bottom lip quivers, and my voice shakes. I used to try to hold it in and wait until I was alone before I would let loose and sob. Nowadays, I cry when I need to cry, and I've let loads of people see my ugly cry face. Because crying provides a release of emotion, the sooner I do it, the sooner I can get to feeling better. Sometimes I warn people, and sometimes I don't, but I have come to a place in my life that if my crying makes others uncomfortable, that's their problem.

I'm a member of a coaching mastermind group with about thirty coaches from all over the world. One of the coaches in my group is a former Argentinian sniper who runs a wolf sanctuary and works with troubled teens. He is chiseled, oozing with masculinity, and a force to be reckoned with. During one of our mastermind exercises, we had to work in pairs and share something about ourselves. I happened to be sitting next to him, so we faced each other and prepared for the exercise. I immediately began to cry, and I apologized to him. He didn't move a muscle, looked me right in the eyes, and asked, "Why are you sorry for crying?"

I replied that I hated to cry, because I thought it was a sign of weakness.

Again, he looked me right in the eyes and stated matter-of-factly, "Maybe you just need to cry."

That statement changed my life. All of the energy I was using to hold in my crying was exhausting. When I need relief, a good cry fits the bill. Why would I continue to avoid it? Like he said, maybe I just needed to cry. Maybe there is a threshold of crying that I need to cross before it can subside. By holding it in, I will never get there. So, now I cry. I cry in front of people. I cry alone. I cry at commercials. I cry when I listen to a podcast about a group of incarcerated teens singing a song about being sorry to their mothers. I cry when I run with my running partners. I cry with my daughter, my son, and my husband. The more I cry, the better I feel, and the more people feel free to connect with me through my crying.

Yes, and Thank You

When I conduct leadership workshops for businesses, I teach about the evolution of feedback and the power of acknowledgment. I show them how I think of acknowledgment and then give them a chance to grab a partner and practice acknowledging them for who they are in the world. It's a beautiful exercise because it shows us how rarely we use acknowledgment, how it requires us to really see the person sitting in front of us, and how we've been conditioned to disbelieve what is being said when we are being acknowledged. I ask them to say, "Thank you," the next time they receive an acknowledgment—and nothing else. It feels pretty awkward at first, but it gets better over time.

I've been trying to address the people who do provide help and support to us with our daughter in that same way. When someone offers to take my daughter for the weekend to give us a break, I reply with "yes" and "thank you." When my running friends ask me to go away for a night to blow off some steam, I say "yes" and "thank you." When I get asked to go grab a pedicure, I say "yes" and "thank you."

The more I can accept the love and support of others, the more love and support comes my way. It's like there is a magnetic force where my willingness to accept help attracts people who actually want to help.

Of course, I have the same voices in my head as everyone else. One of my voices says that these people don't really want to help; they are just offering to be nice. Another one tells me that I cannot accept help because a strong mother can do everything by herself. Yet another whispers the question of what kind of a coach/mother/woman am I that I can't even manage my own life. I try to quiet those voices by listening for the ones that tell me it's okay to ask for help and receive help, to let people love me and my family. I remind myself that I like to help others, so it might be safe to assume that others like to help me. I remember that when I say yes to something, it's because I want to do that thing and I am not trying to please someone, look good in someone else's eyes, or be nice.

When my daughter skipped school and I refused to call her in sick, she called the school and tattled on herself. So, the counselor and dean drove to my house to pick her up. I really struggled with this event, as I am on the school board and worried that there were all sorts of politics that played into them picking up my child. While I thanked them profusely, I still worried what they thought of me. The only way for me to let that event go was to recognize that they wouldn't have picked her up if they didn't want to. It was their way of extending a hand to my daughter. It was their way of showing their love for her. In fact, I now realize that it had very little to do with me at all.

Can I pick up your daughter?

Yes, and thank you.

The Ultimate Barrier

I've noticed that it's hard to accept love and support until I began to love and accept myself. Yes, that's one of those annoying sayings that is cliché and overused. But it's true! As our daughter began her journey into emotional turmoil, I found myself hating myself very often. I was very hard on myself, and I was perpetually concerned with how to fix my daughter, be a better mother, and have both of us emerge stronger than ever before. It wasn't until I looked at myself in the mirror and acknowledged that there is nothing *wrong* with my daughter that I could begin to love and accept myself again too. She is perfect just the way she is, even though she is suffering. When I could accept her as she is, the expectations of being something else melted, and the disappointments and resentments fell away too.

Then a funny thing happened, and I'm still not sure which of these things happened first. I started to feel less pressure, stress, and angst. The voices that told me I was worthless got quieter. I was gentler to myself. The psychological flogging stopped. The crises continue, but I am able to deal with them from a place of peace and calm. Because I can love myself, I can also trust myself to handle anything that comes my way. I can listen to my heart and find a compassionate way through the chaos.

My daughter has plenty of support systems in place with therapists, counselors, teachers, and doctors who are all working to help her. While this is a great thing, I receive lots of feedback from those supporters on a regular basis. When she becomes asthmatic during track practice, the adults call me to come pick her up because they think she is having a panic attack. When her therapist notices that a therapy isn't working, I get called into her office so I can be told that her medications may be interfering with her progress. When she posts something online that is depressing, I receive a text from a parent who is concerned for her safety.

If I became fearful every single time I received a piece of information from someone who is watching out for her, I'd be a constant basket case.

Now, when someone gives me some troubling news about my daughter, I take a deep breath. I tell my brain to take a break and let my heart take the lead. I drop into my body and out of my head. Then I can face what is happening. I can be calm.

Seriously, when my daughter shows up in my room in the night clutching her bleeding arms after she's deliberately sliced her skin to smithereens, I take a deep breath and access my heart. My head will tell me that the sky is falling, she is looking for attention, and I shouldn't enable this behavior. My heart tells me to give her a hug, address the bleeding, chase away the shame she is feeling, and sit with her. I have to assume that she doesn't want to feel this way, and I know that judging her will only make her feel unworthy rather than loved unconditionally.

I also recognize that I have to love myself by taking care of myself. The basics are absolutely critical. I have to eat, sleep, and exercise. I need great friends. I need to spend time petting my cat, dog, and my daughter's five guinea pigs. I choose to enjoy the sunlight on my face, the way the lake looks at sunset, or watching a rare and majestic Kingfisher land on my sailboat. It all adds up. Each moment matters. I can choose to notice the beauty, the peace, the wonder of the world, and, low and behold, I feel really grateful for who I am and the life I am living. If I put myself in my daughter's shoes, I would prefer a mother who is calm and in control rather than one who is frantic, insecure, and prone to panic. By loving myself, I can love my daughter more powerfully.

During a particularly difficult situation when my daughter was feeling suicidal, I caught her running away from school and heading towards a bridge, which she had threatened to jump off of. I have an amazing coach, and she and I discussed what happened. I was distraught as I beat myself up for my daughter's actions, and she made a gentle, but powerful statement.

"Allison, you can't hate yourself into being a better mother."

Indeed.

Steps for Moving Forward:

1. Ask for help. Go ahead. You can do it.
2. Take care of the basics, like eating, sleeping, and showering. Every little moment adds up.

Exercises:

1. Next time somebody asks you if they can do something, give them an answer, like a hug, a cup of coffee, or a prayer. Notice how it feels to let love and support into your life.
2. When you feel as though you might cry, see if you can just let the tears fall. Pay attention to how it feels to let go of the need to hide your emotions.

Chapter 11

Emergencies

One time, there was an emergency while I was in Los Angeles on business. As we were heading into our first meeting of the day, I receive a text from my husband that read:

"I'm with Piper in the ER. She took 20+ Tylenol then told me."

I receive a shot of adrenaline, and instantly felt sick to my stomach. I decided to still go into the meeting while I thought through what I should do, caught in a surreal place where I wasn't in the present moment but also wasn't in the past or future. It was as though I was floating above my own life, watching it unfold before me.

What would life be without emergencies and crises? We try to avoid and minimize them, but they do happen. So, when my husband texted me that he was in the ER with my daughter, I had to slow down and go through my logic loop. Is this an emergency? Is it a crisis? Is it a high priority? Do I need to fly home immediately? Can I wait a day? All of these thoughts in my surreal state came spinning through my mind and had me whirling like a Dervish. For me, it's helpful to have some criteria around what constitutes a true emergency. That way, I am not constantly on high alert or rushing to the rescue for no reason.

Criterion #1: Is this life threatening or dangerous in some way?

This one might seem obvious, but I'd like to elaborate. Having gone through five suicide attempts with my daughter at this point, I am becoming more analytical in my approach to suicide attempts, as they are not all the same.

Each time our daughter has made an attempt to end her life, we've taken her to the ER. Ironically, when you show up at an emergency room, nobody is really all that emergency-like. They first ask for personal information, then take copies of our insurance cards, then ask us to have a seat in the waiting room. Once we are finally brought into the unit, there's a bit more action, like attaching IV's and monitoring her vitals, but everyone is very calm and deliberate. With visions in my mind of stomach pumps and medical personnel running about with crash carts, I decided I needed to revisit my definition of an emergency.

Taking a handful of pills is a serious matter. It can harm my daughter's organs and make her feel sick or experience pain. However, the pills she took were most likely not going to actually kill her, i.e. they are not immediately life-threatening. The second suicide attempt was similar to the first when my daughter swallowed a handful of pills. Only we didn't go racing for the ER this time. Rather, I asked her to pack a bag of clothes she might want to have if she ends up as a patient in a behavioral health unit, I fed the dog and cat, checked on my son, and *then* we went to the ER. There was no reason to get too terribly excited, as we learned from our last visit to the ER that we had time to make decisions and take care of immediate needs before rushing out the door.

Therefore, each consecutive attempt results in us reacting in accordance with the threat. When my husband texted me that acetaminophen poisoning is really serious, that took the danger level up a notch, and I knew it was time to consider trying to get on a flight home. I can tell you that it's much better to begin with assuming a moderate threat level mindset and increase to a more intense threat level than it is to go the other way. Because, sometimes, the threat never increases. This way, we don't overshoot in our response and waste energy on unnecessary worry and hurry, which, in turn, leads to a more peaceful and deliberate approach—just like those ER folks.

Criterion #2: Am I the person who is needed?

As a mom, it's easy to assume that I am the only one who can fix what's broken. When your child falls and skins his or her knee, who do they run to first? When they get scared that a monster is under their bed, who do they beg to sleep in their room? When they go through their first breakup, who do they need a hug from? That's right. M-O-M. Suddenly, I find myself thinking I am the de facto solver of all that has gone awry. But I think there is a better way.

If I can begin by asking myself who is *actually* needed, there is a chance that the answer may not be me. If my daughter has taken a bottle of acetaminophen, there's not much I can do to help her. She needs medical attention. Of course, my daughter wants me to be a part of the picture during these times of crisis but wanting and needing are two very different things. Who she *needs* is a doctor. She only *wants* her mommy.

When I received that text from my husband that he and my daughter were on their way to the ER, my knee-jerk reaction was to find a way to get home and be with them. I was in Los Angeles and they were home in Wisconsin, so the logistics were complicated. And when I was able to take a deep breath and calm down my nervous system—emphasis on the nervous—I could see that my husband was perfectly capable of escorting her to the hospital and managing her care. I wanted to be there with them, and they wanted me there too. But they didn't *need* me to be there to get the care that was required.

And let me just say that this criterion doesn't assuage the guilt of not being able to be there. Us mommies are a guilt-ridden bunch. Every time my daughter self-harms, ends up in the hospital, or falls into the deep, dark hole of depression, I try my best to "fix it" for her. And I have had to come to the painful realization that I may not be who she needs, which doesn't mean that I am not good enough, but it sure can feel that way at times. But if my daughter continues to suffer while in my care, perhaps it's time to consider putting her in someone else's care, even though as I type these words, they make me feel sick to my stomach and my heart breaks just a little more.

Criterion #3: Can I drop what I am doing to be there?

This third criterion is similar to the second, except that it lives more in the world of priorities as opposed to needs and wants, and it goes something like this. If I am going to live my life, I will make plans, obligate myself to things, and take on responsibilities like most adults. I cannot plan my life around whether or not my daughter is going to do something dangerous, simply because we never know when that might happen.

In addition, there is no good time for a crisis.

Several months ago, I was meeting with a client. During my session, my client was pouring her heart and soul out to me. She was emotionally intense and relying on me to hold the safe space for her. Therefore, I could not be interrupted by a text or phone call from my daughter—which is exactly what happened.

As I was working with my client, I received a text from my daughter that she was in trouble. I didn't see the text until I got in my car after my session. I called my daughter, who shared with me that she had taken a handful of ibuprofen pills. As my panic system started gearing up, I realized that I needed to keep her on the phone to assess her condition. It seemed like it was more important for me to keep her on the phone than it was for me to call an ambulance or a neighbor to go check on her—priorities.

There are so many examples of me being in the middle of my life when one of my daughter's crises pops up and demands my attention. Eighteen months ago, I would always choose my daughter's crisis. Month after month, I stopped whatever I was doing to attend to her. Then, at some point, I realized that this wasn't the best approach for either of us. For one, my daughter needs to know that she is strong enough to handle her life. I am always there for her, but she is a courageous and capable young woman who is capable of solving her own issues. Secondly, I have my life to live too, and it isn't healthy for me to live in a constant state of limbo. Both of us need to continue moving forward with our lives and deal with the crises as they arise the best we can.

Emotional Emergencies

There are different kinds of emergencies, and I've noticed that I tend to react to all of them the same way. If my daughter is about to be hit by a car, my body and brain kick into gear to rescue her from physical harm. If my daughter is rejected by her friends, I tend to rescue her from her emotional pain. I really struggle to turn off my "mommy brain" when my children are hurting, whether they are hurting emotionally or physically. Alas, I jump straight into rescue mode before I even have time to think through the consequences of my actions.

When my daughter shares with me that her best friend has turned on her and she no longer has any friends, my "mommy brain" kicks into full gear. Nobody likes to be rejected, as I talked about in a previous chapter. It hurts. It causes fear and worry. Naturally, I don't want my daughter to go through that, so I immediately start solving the issue so she can relax. But the reality is that her being rejected isn't an emergency. Emotionally, rejection is really uncomfortable, but she will get through it. In fact, there is always learning that occurs during adversity. While my rescuing might alleviate my own pain and suffering on her behalf, it only hinders her learning. And then she wonders if she really can get through it after all, since her mother seems set on making sure she fixes the problem.

When I was in L.A. for business, my daughter texted me that she wanted to quit track. She'd only been on the team for about two weeks, and I got an immediate shot of adrenaline. I immediately started spiraling.

Emergency! She'll never follow through with anything.
She'll continue to give up when things get hard.
I must step in and fix it so she can keep going.

But if I can start by taking a deep breath, I can slow down my "mommy brain" and think through all the options. What I decided to do in this case is to let her make the decision after she considered all the people who were involved, like the woman who drives her to practice, her teammates, and her coaches. If, in the end, she still wanted to quit, then I must let her. And when the emotional pain from quitting surfaces, I have to let her experience it. It's a terrible position to be in because I love her so much. I hate to see her suffer.

When I can slow down and separate the physical from the emotional emergencies, I can parent more effectively. Overreacting is not good for our kids, and, of course, neither is underreacting. However, if I had to err on one side, I would begin with underreacting. Underreacting buys me time to truly assess the situation, to determine what kind of emergency I might be dealing with and how serious it is. My "mommy brain" has formed a pattern of making everything into an emergency, so I have a lot of work to do to continue detangling those automated responses.

Sophie's Choice

I also have a son who is twenty months older than my daughter. He loves his little sister, and he knows that her emergencies require his parents to be available to her. But that means he gets left behind a lot. The one thing I know for sure is that you cannot make up that time lost. I am keenly aware of what it's like to have a sibling who gets most of the attention, as my sister suffers from severe emotional issues. Much of my childhood was spent dealing with my sister's different crises, and I frequently felt as though my parents forgot about me because they were so focused on her.

The first time Piper became suicidal, my husband was out of town. I had to drive my daughter to the ER not knowing when I'd be home to take care of my son. While I could reach my son via his cell phone, I felt pulled in two directions. I wanted to stay with my daughter at the hospital and simultaneously be with my son who was home, alone and worried. Each time there is a crisis, I feel this pull. The stress of thinking about my son cooking yet another dinner for himself, doing his homework alone, and making sure all the animals are fed because we are completely consumed with our daughter's needs is overwhelming. Of course, he tells us he understands, but I know from personal experience that it still hurts to be neglected.

As I prepare to take my daughter to another state for a long-term residential care program, I wonder how we will manage this transition. Should we all fly with her? Should I take her by myself? Should my husband go instead? Should both my husband and I go and find someone to stay with our son?

Once again, I feel as though I am standing in front of a buffet of crap sandwiches trying to make a good choice when, the fact is, there aren't any good choices left.

What Kind of Mother...

It's serendipitous that as I was running one morning, I was listening to a podcast called "This American Life." They had a show called "Darned If You Do, Darned If You Don't," and, in it, they shared a story about a mother who needed to send her son to a residential treatment program and the terrible choices she had to make to get him there. As I listened to her story, I had to stop running and sob as I allowed myself to feel the pain of my own decisions regarding the care of my daughter.

What kind of mother am I to send my daughter away?
What kind of mother am I to not be enough for her?
What kind of mother am I to not be able to give her what she needs?

But upon deeper reflection, I think I am exactly the mother my daughter needs right now. She needs a higher level of care than we can provide her, even with multiple inpatient hospital programs, intensive outpatient programs, 504 plans, group therapy, individual therapy, equine therapy, and psychiatrists. As the lethality of her suicide attempts increases, we must take a different approach. The risks are now too high to continue working within systems that have shown little to no success thus far. It is literally insane to continue doing the same thing and expect a different outcome.

So, what kind of mother does my daughter need me to be then?

My daughter needs me to find her that higher level of care that best fits her needs. My daughter needs me to let go of her so she can heal and find a way to live in this world. My daughter needs me to be strong and not question my own worthiness as it relates to being her mom. My daughter needs me to believe in her ability to succeed no matter what. Most importantly, my daughter needs me to love her unconditionally.

My mothering looks different from what I've always assumed a good mother looks like. I have to constantly shatter my assumption so that it does not erode my belief in myself or my relationship with my daughter. My mothering also looks different from what society shows a good mother to be. Again, I have to ignore what someone else's version of a "good mother" might look like since it really doesn't serve me to compare myself to anyone else, even another mother going through similar circumstances.

The best I can do is being the mother my children need me to be.

Words from Piper
The Times I Realized I Wasn't Okay

The first time I realized something was off was when I was a very young age, around four or five years old and I was anxious all the time. I had my own little fantasy place in my head where I would go when I didn't want to deal with the anxiety I would feel or the feeling of being afraid. My dad was an alcoholic when I was a young child. I didn't ever know what was going on, why was my father always getting home late? Why were my parents always yelling at each other? Why was my brother always angry and throwing down? What was going on? What's wrong with these people? I was too young to know any of the answers to these questions so instead of dealing with it, I would escape it. Everything was okay in my world. I had my imaginary friends and my castle with my perfect family, and everything was great in my fantasy world. It started out small. I wouldn't go there very often but as I got older and things in the family got worse, I was always there. I was so bad at this point that I wasn't showing any emotions because I didn't know what was real and what was fake anymore. I finally started seeing a therapist and my dad went to rehab and my brother got his anger under control and my parents weren't fighting anymore and I realized I didn't need that imaginary place anymore.

The second time I realized I wasn't okay was in seventh grade when all the sudden my feelings slowly started to fade away. I didn't know what was happening to me. Why was I suddenly so numb? Nothing was wrong with me. Nothing happened. So why did I feel this way? I was confused. I had no clue what was happening to me. I had friends. I had a good family. I had support. I had a stable life. Why was this happening? It kept getting worse and worse. I was going to school less and less and my appetite began to go away. I self-harmed for the first time on September 28, 2016. I needed to feel something. I was so sick of not feeling anything and I couldn't take it any longer. It was a vicious cycle that started, and I couldn't stop it, so I got help for it. I saw a therapist and I began to improve. Then the suicidal thoughts came. I wanted to die every second of every day. I ended up in the hospital for the first time. I was put on medication and diagnosed with anxiety and depression. I never thought it would happen to me, but it did. And I learned how to deal with it.

The third and final time I realized something was wrong with me was when I felt guilt around eating and food. When I was in eighth grade, I started to feel guilt around food. Like every time I ate, it was bad. My brain told me it was bad to eat, that if I ate, I would gain all this weight, that I would get fat. Of course, it was never true. The truth was that I needed to eat to stay alive, but I was too far down the road of eating disorders to notice that at all. In my second hospitalization I got a feeding tube stuck down my nose all the way to my stomach. It was very uncomfortable, but I found coping skills to eat and not throw it up and not feel *the guilt, so I worked hard and got the feeding tube out after four days. It wasn't fun but I learned a lot from that hospital. I still struggle to eat every day and I struggle with my body image but I'm working on turning that around so I can recover.*

Steps for Moving Forward:

1. Let go of comparing yourself to others, especially in how you handle emergencies. You don't really know what others are going through, so you'll never know the full truth for accurate comparison anyways.
2. Consider what your child needs from you and how it might not be obvious.

Exercises:

1. The next time there is a crisis in the family, take a breath and consider the three criteria of emergency situations.
2. When reflecting on your parenting, try to think of one way to be different from the norm that would improve your relationship with your child, i.e. talk about drugs in a new way, go to an art studio and create something together, or take a trip to a new city for a weekend.

Chapter 12

Impossible Situations

After months of dealing with my daughter's emotional challenges, I got to a point where I had to consider options that I never wanted to have to consider.

If my daughter stayed at home, history told me that she would continue to self-harm and struggle to break her pattern of unhealthy behaviors and thinking. If she went into a long-term residential program, we wouldn't see each other for several months. Short-term hospitalizations hadn't worked. Intensive outpatient programs hadn't helped either. A multitude of different therapy sessions and approaches hadn't worked, either by themselves or combined. Some medications had a positive effect, but others didn't. Any changes to her medication sent her spiraling out of control, attempting suicide, and landing in the ER.

I couldn't bear to watch her suffer anymore. I had to face the reality of two impossible choices: she would stay, or she would go.

D-Day (Drop-off Day)

After a one-hour drive into the Blue Ridge Mountains, I dropped off my daughter at the Wilderness Therapy program, where she will stay for several months without any contact with us. This was the beginning of what will likely become a long-term separation. Chances are that she will go straight into a long-term residential program, which could last for six months to a year, so I had no idea when I might see her again.

Driving to the airport after delivering her to the Wilderness program, I sobbed and let myself feel the pain and anguish of not knowing if this was the right choice and not being able to contact her for several months. I tried to remember how silky her hair feels, how soft her hands are, and how it feels to hold her in my arms. I try to remember how she looks at me, so I never forget her face.

As my plane took off from Asheville, the golden spindles of love that connect my heart to hers felt like they'd been pulled to their max. I cried as I watched the Blue Ridge Mountains disappear, imagining my daughter somewhere down there in the woods, scared, angry, and receiving an enormous dose of reality. When I arrived at the Charlotte airport, I glanced at my boarding pass for my next flight to Chicago and saw a time of 4:20p.m. With about thirty minutes to kill, I grabbed dinner and hit the bathroom. I settled in at my gate and enjoyed my pizza with headphones on as I binge-watched the remaining episodes of Riverdale I had downloaded for the trip. When 4:20 p.m. arrived, I noticed the gate screen no longer displayed the information about my flight. I approached the gate agent to see what happened and she kindly informed me that the flight had already departed. I mistakenly assumed the flight boarded at 4:20p.m. But really, that was the departure time.

In other words, I sat at my gate with people all around me boarding my flight and never even noticed. I was clearly not in my right mind.

Stunned that I had missed my flight whilst sitting at the gate the entire time it was boarding, I wandered to the customer service desk with tears in my eyes. Thankfully, I was quickly rebooked on the next flight.

Still kicking myself for making such a dumb mistake, I decided to call my husband and teetered between laughing and crying as I recounted the story for him. Unfortunately, my new flight was delayed over and over for the next five hours and eventually was canceled altogether. Alas, I had to spend another night in North Carolina and there was nothing I could do about it. It felt cruelly ironic that I couldn't be with my daughter *nor* with my son and husband. I was stuck in travel purgatory.

Thinking about it later, it was as if my heart and my daughter's heart had conspired with the universe to remain close to each other for just one more night. I was uncharacteristically calm about being held captive in an airport for what turned out to be seven hours total and then having to stand in line for another thirty minutes to be rebooked on a flight the next day. I was actually peaceful as I reserved a cheap room at a nearby motel so I could at least get a few hours of sleep before I had to return to the airport the following morning.

Deep down, something inside me had surrendered. I was allowing life to happen to me, letting myself float along with the current.

So, what have I learned through this whole journey with my daughter?

I've learned that letting go of things outside of my control is a great tool for staying calm and peaceful. I've learned that when flights get delayed or canceled, it may just be an opportunity to stay closer to my daughter for just a few more hours give our heart spindles a chance to repair a bit before being stretched again. I've learned that I don't *have* to do anything and that it can be nice to take a break from life. I've learned that I love my daughter more than words can describe and I will stop at nothing to get her the care she needs. I've learned that she is a strong and courageous young woman. I've learned that my husband and I are partners who will catch each other, no matter what. I've learned that my son is an amazing young man who is keenly aware of all the moving parts and will pitch in to help and support. And I've learned that my family *will* get through this. We may not be unscathed, but it will be worth it to get through this together.

Aftermath

When I finally landed in Chicago the next day, I was once again overcome with emotion.

As I was waiting to exit the airplane, I noticed a little girl about two years old standing on her father's lap. She was pointing at the overhead light with her chubby, little toddler fingers, and I found myself yearning for the days when my little girl only needed a hug and her blankie to feel better. I grieved as I thought about how hard life had become since the days of pigtails and training wheels. The nostalgia of all the hopes and dreams I had for her were like a sword to the heart, and this little girl represented all that was lost to us.

Driving home brought on another wave of dread as I thought about entering our home and not having my daughter there. I thought about going into her room and how it would feel knowing she'd be gone for at least six months. I wondered if I would forget that she wasn't home and call her name for dinner. I worried about how empty the house would feel without her.

As my husband, son, and I ate dinner together that evening, we all felt both exhaustion and relief. The worst was now over. The Band-Aid had been ripped off. Our energy was low, and we had resigned ourselves to the reality that she wasn't going to be around for a long time. We were just being together.

The next morning, I came downstairs to find my husband sitting at the kitchen counter with his head in his hands. When I asked him what was wrong, he said, "The damn basement is flooded."

Literally and figuratively, when it rains, it pours. I continued to get ready to go to the gym and made the decision that I needed a workout more than I needed to pump water out of the basement. It was simply too overwhelming for me to think about the flooding. And it became another moment of surrender to life. I was calm and peaceful. My workout was great. I didn't worry about the basement the whole time. My body and soul needed that workout and fulfilling that need allowed me to come home and deal with the mess.

We Are in the Way

While the Wilderness program does not allow us to contact our daughter directly, we do speak to her therapist every week. After only two days of our daughter being in the program, we had our first call scheduled. The program gives us and our daughter a specific set-up for our initial letters to each other. Our letter to her is supposed to detail why she is there and what we hope she gets out of the program, and she is supposed to let us know how she feels about being there. We received her letter to us about fifteen minutes before our scheduled call with her therapist. It was a scathing attack on me for how I'd given up on her and how much she hated it there. She vowed to kill herself and stated that she had a plan to do so. She ranted about how she was making progress at home, how she was forging new friendships, and how we'd ripped her away from all that was good in her life and sent her away to be "fixed."

I felt adrenaline rush through my veins and my amygdala start firing up. My mommy brain was getting ready to rescue her, but this time I couldn't do that.

When we jumped on the call with her therapist, she started by asking if we'd read our daughter's letter to us. She informed us that this letter was totally normal and was affectionately referred to as the "bail letter." In other words, all teens beg their parents to come save them when they first get to the program.

My blood pressure dropped, and I was able to breathe normally again. She then informed us that our daughter was going through all the normal stages of trying to gain control by refusing to eat or drink and not talking to anyone. After two full days on-site, our daughter was already making progress and admitting to making threats because she thought they would send her home if she did.

It now makes perfect sense that most programs do not allow contact between parents and their child. Our natural pattern of behavior as parents is part of the problem. My body literally starts pumping adrenaline when my daughter is hurting. She is seeking to be rescued, and I am more than willing to rescue her. As a relatively self-aware woman who knows all about enabling behaviors, I was surprised that I couldn't recognize my enabling behavior with my own daughter.

Without having me available to constantly rescue her, she'll be forced to find a new pattern. She'll also be given time to practice her new patterns without any setbacks from unsuspecting do-gooders, like family and friends. While it was hard for me to imagine how separating a child from her loving family would be helpful, I now understand.

We were in each other's way.

What Now?

My daughter is gone, and I won't have any contact with her other than a weekly letter for about two months. I feel as though I have given her away, and my heart grieves the loss almost as though I have lost her forever. Logically, I know I will see her again, but my heart has been broken by the loss of not being able to see her, talk with her, and be with her every day. I have made the conscious choice to feel these intense feelings of grief and anguish. I've let them surface and sat with them on purpose. I've sobbed, cried, moaned, and rocked myself through them.

As I've surrendered to reality, I've found a new peace. I can sleep, for the most part. I can do my work. I can continue with my daily obligations. Sometimes I am overcome with sadness. Other times, I feel hopeful that my daughter is going to get better. And yet other times, I almost forget what is happening. I don't force anything anymore, and it's led to a radical acceptance of what is. I can choose all sorts of ways to deal with this reality, and I have chosen to feel my feelings. This is not path for the wimpy, as it demands a mental and emotional fortitude to power through these feelings. But I am finding that the lasting peace this path provides is well worth the discomfort.

The day before we left for the Wilderness program, my daughter and I were both feeling unsettled. I suggested that we buy matching rings or bracelets that we could wear to feel connected while we had to be far apart. We found two identical, orange, beaded bracelets. That evening, we laid them out together under the moonlight to absorb positive energy from the universe. We talked about how we would use our bracelets to send love to each other until we could see each other again, and I remarked how the bracelet is a wrap style, so it's like a hug for our wrists.

I wear my bracelet every single day. I wear it to bed. I wear it to the gym. I wear it regardless of whether or not it matches my outfit. I wear it because I promised my daughter I would. I wear it because I trust my daughter is wearing hers too and remembering how much I love her. I wear it because it represents our love for each other. And I will continue to wear my bracelet until the moment I see my daughter again.

Words from Piper
What I Am
Lonely
Worthless
Unloved
That's what I am
I am nothing
Literally nothing
I'm different
I'm the weird one
The depressed one
The one no one wants
The one people are scared of
Lonely
Worthless

Unloved
That's what I am

"Bail" Letter from Wilderness Therapy (Day 1)

I hate it here. Why did you ship me off like this? Why couldn't you trust me? I just wanted to go to school and be with my friends, but you forced me to be here and I'm mad about that. I didn't think it was going to be this bad, but it is, and I would rather be anywhere but here. This place makes me want to die and I have a plan to do it so, I am sorry, but I can't be here anymore. I would able to handle like if I was at home or in residential, but I can't do it here. Everyone sucks and I want to go home and be a family again. I want to have my friends back and my life back. Why can't you give me a chance? I loved you and I though you weren't going to give up on me, but you did. You shipped me off when I was trying to work on myself. I was actually going to try this time, but I'm done now. Bye.

Steps for Moving Forward:

1. Surrender to reality and let it carry you. The surrender can be intentional or subconscious. Once you surrender, the load is immediately lightened.

2. Feel your feelings. Allow them to surface regardless of the timing. There's never a good time to fall apart, sob, and make the ugly cry face. If it needs to happen, let it.

Exercises:

1. When negative emotions arise, try leaning into them. This means if you have a thought about something that stirs fear,

anger, or sadness in you, continue moving into the feelings. It might hurt or cause discomfort, but your emotional muscle will gain strength each time you do it.

2. Practice gratitude. Verbalize or write down at least one thing that you can be grateful for each day. If you're really brave, try to find gratitude for the painful situation you may be experiencing and the opportunities that might arise from it.

Chapter 13

Parenting Conundrums

t occurred to me only after my daughter left for Wilderness therapy that having a child who suffers from emotional and behavioral issues requires a higher level of parenting. Just when I had let go of my guilt and shame for having a child who doesn't operate like other kids, I am faced with the notion that I cannot be casual in my parenting. In fact, I have to overcome all of my own bad habits that I have developed over fifteen years of being a mom.

But I don't feel put out by my daughter or resentful that her issues require extra work from me. Instead, I feel like my journey into self-awareness and personal intelligence never ends. Just as I was thankful for having an alcoholic husband because it forced me to learn how to be a better person, I am grateful for the challenges I have faced as a mother with a child who is currently struggling and the growth it has required me to embrace.

After leaving my daughter at the Wilderness program, I went through a deep, dark period of despair. I never wanted to be away from my daughter for months without contact, but I'm doing it. I dropped her off at a camp in the woods and left. In that place of pain and hurt and sadness, I learned that I *can* do it. I *can* handle the fears and the worries. I don't like it, but I can do it. I also learned that I need to up my parenting game, because I have some patterns that need breaking. I had to do some digging of my own to get to a place where I could focus on my behavior and make some discoveries.

Now, would I recommend that every parent ditch their kids for months to become better parents? Heck no! It just happens to be my journey and I must embrace that reality.

But I'm Mom

Darn it all if I don't have to learn the same lessons over and over again!

When I started going to Al-Anon, I discovered that I was enabling the alcoholics in my life to behave badly. I even went so far as to clean up their messes. In Al-Anon, I learned how to create and defend boundaries with my loved ones, and I thought I was all done learning about boundaries. Imagine my surprise when I recognized that my daughter's bad behavior has been tolerated by none other than yours truly. All of our behavior is a means to an end. My daughter needed her emotional discomfort to go away, and she needed someone to fix it for her. Enter mommy.

I'll fix it. I'll solve. I'll make a plan. I'm her mom!

Not surprisingly, my tendency to be a people pleaser results in not being a big fan of accountability when it comes to my kids, so I repeatedly let my daughter off the hook. When I ask her to do something like clean her room and she negotiates a different deadline and then fails to make it happen, my tendency is to let her get away with it. The problem is that when I tolerate this behavior, it sends unintentional signals about my beliefs in her. It tells my daughter that I don't think she's capable of cleaning her room in a timely fashion, that my requests aren't really serious. I don't honor her by letting her skate by without fulfilling her obligations. Her workarounds for her emotions, like isolating herself, giving up, and self-harming, were developed in an environment where they elicited the responses that she was looking for from the people around her.

Make no mistake, this isn't pathological or manipulative so much as simple human nature. Her problem is feeling overwhelmed by her emotions, which she solves by escaping or being rescued. Since I love to mother, care for, and nurture her, I am quick rush in and make her hurt go away.

I can clearly see that my habit in parenting is rescuing. I didn't realize how much I rescued, saved, and fixed things for my daughter to spare her emotional distress. I also recognize that my rescuing relieves my own discomfort, which isn't terribly helpful for my daughter. While I know I can withstand copious amounts of pain and suffering, I cannot seem to translate that skill into withstanding witnessing pain and suffering in my daughter. I know from my own personal and professional work that we learn so much when we are challenged, so it is ironic that I want to clear a nice, clean path for my daughter with no challenges, no struggles, and easy cruisin' all the way.

As she hikes, camps, and survives in the woods, I imagine she is being challenged quite a bit. She's away from her family and friends with no contact. She is with people she doesn't know well. She's in a state she's never been to before. She has never had to make a fire or cook over it. She doesn't really know how to pitch a tent without help. And, oh yeah, she has to face all of the fears and frustrations that come with being her.

But just like waiting nine months to meet the baby growing inside you, I cannot wait to find out what she's like now.

Re-Entry

With my daughter gone for a few months, all I can seem to think about is what things will be like when she comes home.

How will things be different?
How do we set her up for success?
What should I be doing now to prepare?

All this future-focused thinking is part distraction, part catastrophizing, and part self-awareness developing. I find it interesting that my son and husband see my daughter's issues as her own and don't see a need to change themselves. I, on the other hand, have a different perception. I see that she has developed some troubling behavior patterns that are working for her. Because we live in the same house and spend the most time with her, we must somehow be rewarding her unhealthy coping skills.

In other words, we all have our own issues and we can all raise the bar for our own behavior if we want to support both ourselves and each other.

When you live with an alcoholic, you learn that the whole family must adjust if they want the alcoholic to succeed. That adjustment, while difficult, and at times painful, is the key to unburdening ourselves in many other aspects of our lives.

For example, I was able to identify bad behavior and stop tolerating it. When my husband would show up drunk at home, I would call him a cab and have him taken to the hotel of his choice. This was very difficult for my family. We never knew how he would show up or when the next crisis would pop up. It was interesting how my other relationships outside our immediate family shifted as well.

My mother and sister have a long history of bad behavior with me, but because of the work I had done to set boundaries with my husband, I was able to create boundaries with them too. I was able to minimize the things in my life that drained me of energy and protect the things that gave me energy. And I slowly felt more peace in my life.

Just like I discovered with the work I did with my husband, I suspect that I will learn some powerful insights by changing my perspectives on parenting, and those will likely translate to other surprises.

I've already experienced one 'ah-ha' moment when we received our daughter's angry letter begging us to come get her. Had she been within driving distance, I would have driven to see her. Could I have talked to her over the phone, I would have called her—without thinking twice. My mommy brain would have kicked in and off I'd go to rescue her from her pain. As we dealt with that letter from afar, I realized that my first reaction was to fix something. Again, this is what I did with the other loved ones in my life, so I shouldn't be too surprised that I also do it with my own daughter.

My love for others gets in my way at times. If I am emotionally in tune with my daughter and feel her pain, I am more likely to find the source of the problem and make it go away. As I ponder what will need to change when she eventually comes home, I find myself afraid to set rules and hold her accountable. When I dig deep, I find behind that hesitation an assumption that my daughter might not love me if I discipline her. Even as I write those words, I know better. But there it still is, a small flame of fear that my daughter will reject me if I give her boundaries and structure.

And, as always, it's complicated. Because my daughter self-harms and has attempted suicide several times, it often feels like enforcing certain boundaries could be downright dangerous. But I suspect that if our family can learn how to agree on boundaries and enforce them from a place of love rather than fear, we will all uncover just how capable we are.

I remember someone once telling me a story about fencing around an elementary school playground. After having fencing for a while, the school decided to remove it so the kids could have a bigger area to play. Before the fence was removed, the kids utilized the whole area, playing right along the fence (their boundary). When that fence/boundary was gone, the kids all congregated in the middle of the playground, using much less square footage. The theory is that kids like boundaries and feel safer and more secure when they know where those boundaries are.

So, as we plan for our daughter to come home, I'm still not sure what exactly boundaries and discipline will look like, but I do know that I will have to define where the "fence" is and let her know that it's staying—with plenty of deep breaths along the way.

Pattern Exhaustion

After my daughter's first week in the Wilderness program, we received a call from her therapist. Just like our first call, about fifteen minutes prior, we received digital copies of letters she wrote to us that week. There were four letters all over the map emotionally.

One letter apologized for her first letter that had expressed her anger towards us. The second letter shared how much she missed us and begged us to find a way to call her. The third was about how hard she was going to work to get through the program. The fourth was a desperate cry for help detailing how she had run away from the group and self-harmed four times. After reading these letters, I was fully panicked about her condition.

When we got on the call with her therapist, I let her know how troubling the letters were. The therapist shared that my daughter had really struggled during her first week in the program. She was isolating herself, not engaging with the group, and making sure all the adults knew how unhappy she felt. On her fifth day, my daughter escalated her attempts to be rescued by charging the staff and trying to cut herself with parts of a mechanical pencil she had broken off. Each episode was met with a caring, but firm, enforcement of their boundaries. The staff reiterated to her that they were there to keep her safe, and then made sure she was supervised at all times. Nobody rescued her. Nobody made her feel better. Nobody fixed her predicament. They cared, they helped, but they did not fix.

The therapist continued to explain this was the part of the program referred to as the "pattern exhaustion" phase. They allow the girls to show the therapists their behavior patterns that have been working for them so far. However, those patterns do not work in the Wilderness program. The kids try to get resolution with the same behaviors and keep being met with a gentle, but firm, no-tolerance approach for bad behavior.

Her therapist told us that we all have the ability to self-soothe, and the sooner the girls figure out how to calm themselves, the better. It made me think of the days of baby sleep training when I would let my daughter cry for a while before I would go in to pacify her. After only a few crying spells, she did figure out how to soothe herself and fell asleep quickly.

By the sixth morning of the Wilderness program, my daughter had turned a corner. She was no longer desperate and appeared calm and compliant. By noon that day, her therapist met with her for an individual session and remarked on how well she did. They uncovered all sorts of buried beliefs and assumptions, and my daughter was now willing to try a different approach to life. During the session, my daughter could see the other girls outside, laughing and having a good time. My daughter's therapist looked at my daughter and said, "You deserve to have joy and you belong with them."

When my daughter left the session, she immediately engaged with the girls and was smiling and experimenting with belonging. I think my heart almost swelled out of my chest with pride and joy when the therapist told us about this session.

Another interesting phenomenon about my daughter's time away is that I cannot get enough of her therapist talking about her. I wanted her to talk to me all evening. It was so lovely to see my daughter through someone else's eyes, particularly someone who understood my daughter. It was like a salve for my heart. After our discussion, I received two photos of my daughter from the therapist, and it was striking how she exuded pure joy in these photos. Something had shifted inside her; she was different.

Words from Piper
Letter from Wilderness (Day 4)

I want to see you guys so badly. I am trying so hard to get out and succeed here so I can be in a place where I can communicate with you. It wouldn't be that bad here if I could hear your voice. I am going to ask for one phone call with you for my birthday. I just need that right now, really need it. I can't say it enough, but I love you guys so dang much and I really miss you so much. Every day I miss you more and more. I just wanted to thank you for everything you've done for me and keeping me alive. I love you guys and I really hope I can get out soon. I'll work really hard. I love you guys.

Steps for Moving Forward:

1. Our behaviors are a means to getting our needs met. Explore your own patterns of behaviors, both positive and negative. Then decide what to do about the ones that are no longer serving you.

2. Because a family dynamic is created by everyone in it, when one member is struggling, it is helpful to analyze the family as a whole. If you have a child who is exhibiting bad behavior, then try stepping back and examining how each member reacts to see how the pattern might be reinforced.

Exercises:

1. Pick one pattern in your life that really bothers you. Uncover the need that it fulfills. Take full responsibility for getting your own needs met in healthy and positive ways and work

towards breaking the unhealthy pattern and replacing it with a healthy alternative.

2. If you are a fixer, rescuer, and solver, try letting your child fix their own problem. Notice how you can still care for them without fixing their issue.

Epilogue

What Now?

I t's been six months since I wrote the first chapter of this book. So much has changed, and yet, we still face similar issues and challenges every day.

But, while our daughter continues to struggle, she is also making significant growth. While our family has taken a beating, we are also coming together, healing our relationships, and plowing a path forward. While our marriage has been severely tested, we are agreeing to give each other lots of space, patience, and understanding. Sometimes we do well, and, others, well, not so much.

Hope

If you have a child—or any loved ones—who suffers greatly, I think it's normal to wonder if this life is just too damn hard for them. Of course, I don't want to lose my daughter—ever! But there have been times when I wondered how much more she could endure. And how much more I could take.

Thankfully, the wondering never erases my hope.

Because there *is* hope. For all the setbacks, relapses, running away, food and water strikes, self-harming, disturbing posts, and terrifying threats, she's still alive and doing better than she once was. Life still isn't easy for her, but she allows herself moments of joy that she soaks up. She has learned to be present, so she now finds respite from the darkness more often. She practices what she's learned; she's shifted her mindset.

I have hope for all of us. I now know that my marriage may not be in tip-top shape, but it has survived these troubling times. I know that we can repair our family relationships, even the ones we thought were too far gone. I know that I can handle way more than I ever imagined. I know that life has lots of ups and downs, and I can allow them to happen. I know that fear, blame, and shame are joy bullies.

Hope, to me, means knowing that I am—we are—going to be okay.

Clarity

These tough times have also provided clarity about what is truly important. For instance, I wanted to be viewed as a good mother and that had me focusing on others' perceptions rather than myself and my children. I thought hiding what was happening to Piper stemmed out of integrity, but hiding meant I was ashamed or embarrassed of her behavior, and I know too well the costs of growing up with shame and judgment as parenting techniques. I had to push aside my fears of what others might think of me in order to get the help my daughter needed.

Now, I am clear in my intentions whenever I share our story. If it seems as though our story will serve someone, I tell it. If I need to share in order to get help, I do. If I'm struggling and require support, I find my people and speak my truth in that moment.

I used to think if I told one person, I would have to tell everyone when, actually, I still have significant control around who I choose to tell. I have to accept that what they do with the information is out of my control. Most of the time, I have found love, support, camaraderie, help, resources, and deep connections.

I also thought that if I told people what was happening in our family, they would blab and it would become a game a telephone in which everyone would know some inaccurate version of our story. To some extent, this is true and does happen. The difference is that I am now clear that I don't care. The people who are going to be helpful will come forward and give us a hand. The people who are interested in gossip will gossip. The only way it affects us is if they want to support us. If not, it's not my problem. This epiphany and commitment to not worry about it has been such a huge relief for me.

What I've Learned

Instead of trying to create beautiful prose around the wisdom I've gained through this journey, here's a list—with bullet points. I've learned to:

- Cry when I need to cry.
- Quit worrying about making people uncomfortable.
- Love unconditionally.

- Allow life to happen.
- Let go of control.
- Accept reality.
- Reframe my daughter's struggles.
- Be aware of how much I care what other people think.
- Be less judgmental.
- Accept kindness from anyone and everyone.
- Be okay with awkward and messy.
- Accept I am a good enough mother.
- Honor my daughter's choices, even when they cause her to suffer.
- Stop rescuing her.
- Put the relationship before the task.
- Use breathing as a means to beat back anxiety and panic.

When you think about it, I'm the lucky one. My daughter taught me all of those things. She has been a blessing to her family and friends. People fall in love with her because of her immense kindness and gentleness. I've learned that she isn't "broken," but, instead, a gift to all who connect with her.

The most important thing I have learned is that I was chosen to be her mother for a reason. She requires a strength, love, and conviction that a lesser woman could never muster. My daughter has awakened in me a power and force I didn't even realize I had. And when I am being her mother, I am in awe of what I can do. I used to feel like our daughter needed to be fixed when, in actuality, she is the one who fixed me.

Life

I am often struck by just how difficult life can be. And when I fight what life throws at me, I only end up suffering more. It has only been through surrendering and allowing life to unfold as it will that I have found peace. Worry is a dark fog that overtakes everything and makes it difficult to see the truth. As Piper would say, worrying is just "future tripping."

I don't know what is in Piper's future, nor do I have any idea about my own. That's okay.

I know that today was a good day. Piper won "Student of the Week" at her school. My son did well on his AP test. The laundry got done. My clients were great. I had lunch with some beautiful friends. I can permit myself to enjoy these things to their fullest because I've expanded my emotional range. Just like a singer who can hit the highest and lowest notes, I can feel exquisite joy and incredible darkness. Even though my lows are lower, my highs are also higher.

As life moves on, I can rest confidently in my own capability to handle whatever happens. I'm better equipped. I no longer live in constant fear and stress and dread. When things are going well, I don't hold back my enjoyment for fear of when the other shoe is going to drop. I don't feel guilty for experiencing happiness, nor do I feel guilty for sitting in my sadness. Life is so much better when I allow it to develop. There is ease and flow, here, in this total surrender.

Words from Piper

Here I am. 14 years old. I'm writing this from my residential treatment facility. I've been here 6 months since I graduated from my Wilderness Program at the end of July. This has been the hardest thing I've ever gone through. I've made a lot of mistakes. I've run away, self-harmed, and overdosed. Making mistakes doesn't mean you're going backwards. It means you're growing.

When I was in a dark place, I used to think "I'm fine" or "dying young is the right decision". My last time going home for a visit, I made a big mistake. The thing I felt this time was different. Shame! Guilt! Regret! I thought "this was a big mistake. What do I do now?" I lied about it. I knew it was wrong. I knew I wasn't okay. And, believe it or not, that is progress.

I'm sharing my story to help other young teens like me. We are all worthy of love, help, happiness, and acceptance. Love one another. Nurture one another. Befriend one another. The best gift I've been given is my mom's unconditional love for me.

"I'm telling my story not because it's unique, but because it isn't." - Malala

Acknowledgments

'd like to acknowledge my daughter, Piper. As you now know, she's an extraordinary young woman. She's showing all of us how to be more courageous. She tells her story from a place of abundance because she wants others to know they aren't alone. While it's uncommon for teens to think of others before themselves, Piper is willing to be brave and share her story focused solely on how it can help others. Thank you, Piper, for being my daughter and teaching the world to embrace discomfort.

When the idea of co-creating a book popped into my mind, I immediately called my book coach, Ruth Klein. She helped me write my first book ("Think Possible"), and I just knew she would walk this journey with both my daughter and me. While this was, at times, quite painful to write, Ruth believed in us and encouraged us to put our story out there for others.

Once we were done writing, I wanted to find a special person to edit it for us. Enter Aubrey Kosa. While it was daunting to have someone else read our story, Aubrey quickly reassured us that she loved what we were doing and wanted to help put this book into the hands of readers. Not only did she understand our voice, she helped us articulate our points more clearly and smoothly.

After publishing my previous book with Morgan James, I felt safe asking them to consider this special book that was very close to my heart. They were wonderfully compassionate and made us feel they would treat our creation with great care.

Finally, I want to thank my husband and son, who stood by us as we waded into this endeavor. When we share our story, it impacts all four of us. They know that our dirty laundry will be aired, and they only see love for what Piper and I have created. My boys have been unwavering in their support of our work.

About the Authors

Allison Garner is a leadership coach, business consultant, engineer, and author. She has a Bachelor's in Chemical Engineering, Master's in Business Administration, and is a Certified and Credentialed Professional Coach. After serving as an engineer for 20 years in the oil industry with her last position as Vice President of an engineering consulting firm and one of the world's experts in aromatics extraction, she founded her own leadership coaching and consulting practice, Align Coaching LLC, in 2015. In addition to sitting on multiple boards and advisory committees, she has been an elected School Board member for 9 years serving as its Treasurer, Vice President, and President. She has been a resident of Oshkosh, WI since 2000 where she lives on the beautiful inland Lake Winnebago. She published her first book, Think Possible: The Light and Dark Side of Never Running Out of Ideas, in 2019 with Morgan James Publishing.

Piper Garner is a high school student. At age 12, Piper started to experience mental health struggles and was diagnosed with depression. Her three year journey to mental wellness included three months in wilderness therapy and one year at a residential boarding school. She's passionate about animals, nature, and connecting with people without judging them.

References

Chapter 3

Twenge, J. M. (2017). iGen: Why Today's Super-Connected Kids Are Growing Up Less Rebellious, More Tolerant, Less Happy – and Completely Unprepared for Adulthood. New York: Atria Books.

Twenge, J. M., 2017, 'Making iGen's Mental Health Issues Disappear', Psychology Today, accessed 4 February 2018, https://www.psychologytoday.com/blog/our-changing-culture/201708/making-igens-mental-health-issues-disappear.